The Light that Puts an End to Dreams

Other works by Susan Sherman:

Poetry

Areas of Silence

With Anger / With Love

Women Poems Love Poems

We Stand Our Ground
(with Kimiko Hahn & Gale Jackson)

Barcelona Journal

Casualties of War

Essays, Poems, Short Fiction

The Color of the Heart:
Writing from Struggle and Change, 1959-1990

Memoir

America's Child:
A Woman's Journey Through the Radical Sixties

Translation

Shango de Ima
(An adaptation from Spanish of a play
by Cuban playwright Pepe Carril)

The Light that Puts an End to Dreams

New & Selected Poems by

Susan Sherman

featuring a suite of poems for
Sor Juana Inés de la Cruz

Photographs by Joséphine Sacabo

Introduction by Margaret Randall

WingsPress

San Antonio, Texas
2012

The Light that Puts an End to Dreams © 2012 by Susan Sherman.
Introduction © 2012 by Margaret Randall.

Cover and interior photographs © 2012 by Joséphine Sacabo.
Used by permission of the artist.
Author portrait photograph © 2008 by Colleen McKay.

Print Edition ISBN: 978-0-916727-94-9

Ebook editions:
ePub ISBN: 978-1-60940-222-8
Kindle ISBN: 978-1-60940-223-5
Library PDF ISBN: 978-1-60940-224-2

Wings Press
627 E. Guenther
San Antonio, Texas 78210
www.wingspress.com

All Wings Press titles are distributed to the trade by
Independent Publishers Group • www.ipgbook.com

Library of Congress Cataloging-in-Publication Data:

Sherman, Susan, 1939-
   [Poems. Selections]
   The light that puts an end to dreams : new & selected poems / by Susan Sher-
man ; photographs by Josephine Sacabo ; introduction by Margaret Randall.
      p. cm.
   Includes bibliographical references.
   "featuring a suite of poems for Sor Juana Inés de la Cruz."
   ISBN 978-0-916727-94-9 (pbk. : alk. paper) -- ISBN 978-1-60940-222-8
(ePub eBook) -- ISBN 978-1-60940-223-5 (Kindle eBook) -- ISBN 978-1-
60940-224-2 (library pdf eBook)
   I. Sacabo, Josephine. II. Randall, Margaret, 1936- III. Title.
PS3569.H434A6 2012
811'.54--dc23
                                    2011046746

Q: But what shall we dream of when everything becomes visible?

A: We'll dream of being blind.

—Paul Virilio
(Interviewed by Louise K. Wilson)

Contents

Long Division

Cantos for Elegua

The Light that Puts an End to Dreams

Introduction

Susan Sherman has been a pivotal figure in late twentieth and early twenty-first century U.S. American culture for over forty years, with a solid body of poetry, theater, essay, and memoir. She has been involved in many important movement and progressive political efforts of her time, often in the vanguard or on the front lines. She produced a magazine that published some of the finest work and documented many of the events in the '60s and again in the '80s and '90s, always making the connection between thought and action. And she ran a storefront locale that became an important New York focus for alternative learning and activism, art and organizing. But for reasons I will explore in this introduction to her first comprehensive collection of poems, her work has not achieved the notice it so richly deserves.

Who is this woman with the engaging smile and warm embrace? I'll give some of the basics of Susan's life in her own words. This is from her part in a three-way conversation (with Gale Jackson and Kimiko Hahn) that opens their 1988 book, *We Stand Our Ground*:

> *I like the word "origins" because to me it means not only your childhood or your roots (your starting point in time) but what continues, what makes your work, your daily life possible [...] I grew up in Los Angeles during the 40s and 50s... When I finished college in 1961 I came to New York and didn't return to California for over 17 years.*
>
> *Berkeley in the late '50s and early '60s—the Beat Generation, the San Francisco Renaissance, North Beach, poetry, the "sexual revolution" and my first real experiences*

with sex and love—unfortunately then not the same; my first relationship with a woman; the House Un-American Activities Committee police "riots"; the first time I saw a real alternative to the life I had known....

New York, 1961, '62, '63—poetry readings at the Deux Megots, Le Metro, writing and directing plays at the Hardware Poets Theatre...the riots in '63, '64, the episodes of disassociation, panic... The struggle to survive. The mid 60s—Angry Arts Against the War, the Free University, the Alternate University, the founding of the first series of IKON, "coming out" in 1961 and then slowly retreating in and then "coming out" again. The trips to Cuba in 1967 and '68—and consciousness of a reality totally separate from any I had recognized before—loss of job, ulcer, loss of magazine, turning that loss into intense political involvement and commitment and creativity, not born from, but energized by anger—as my poetry had been, from personal anger, from a consciousness of my parents' brutality years before.

The '70s—Chile, breakup of first long relationship, the 5th St. Women's Building, the Lesbian/feminist movement, the silence of years that were a pulling together as well as a breaking apart; Sagaris, a bad automobile accident. The '80s—Nicaragua, the new IKON, a new relationship. All that I remember, all that I have forgotten. My origins, what made me, make me what I am today.

This, then, is the bedrock, some of the personal history that has shaped the thinker and writer. Today Susan teaches at Parsons (The New School). One or another of her close to a dozen off-off Broadway plays is still occasionally produced. And these days she writes the stunning poetry of maturity. Her memoir, *America's Child: A Woman's Journey Through the Radical Sixties,* was recently published to great acclaim, and a collection of short fiction,

Nirvana on Ninth Street—really the memoir of a place: a particular neighborhood in New York City's Lower East Side—is in the works.

When historians of the 1960s, '70s or '80s look at some of New York's seminal grass-roots cultural events, they find that Susan played a central role in their organization. And many of us continue to read her groundbreaking essays on philosophy and popular culture. Her suite of essays, "The Tyranny of Form," "The ABC of Madness—The Legacy of Derrida," and "The Obscure Subject of Desire: The Despair of Jacques Lacan," is still among the best analyses of late twentieth century manipulation of aesthetics and media around. I have often said that had Susan been a man she would have been called a philosopher; as a woman she has had to settle for lesser titles.

Her influential journal, IKON, enjoyed two runs: the editorial mission of the first published in the middle to late '60s, could be summed up in its logo: "Creativity and Change." In Susan's own words it featured "art as an impetus to action, not divorced from, but irrevocably part of our involvement in this world, this present moment in which we find ourselves." This has been a constant in Susan's political commitment and in her art; indeed, many of her efforts have demonstrated the connection between art and social change in profound and innovative ways.

The first IKON was dedicated to breaking longstanding artistic taboos—holdovers from academic strictures and McCarthyism—and a certain U.S. insularism that claimed artists and writers could not write objectively about people they knew or about their own work, that art must be seen as separate from the context in which it was created.

That first IKON ceased publication when poverty, hardship and the political repression of the era proved too much for people like Susan, for whom the work was always a labor of love. But it was reborn in 1982, within the intensity of feminism's second wave. This run showcased women's work. In contrast with its larger format magazine-style predecessor, the issues of the new series were book-sized volumes; but their brilliant graphic design—always serving creative expression rather than the other way around—continued to reflect Susan's imaginative artistic and editorial direction. Although solidly within the feminist tradition, and publishing women's work almost exclusively, IKON was never arbitrarily separatist (here again, she bucked the trend of the moment, defying those who failed to understand her more complex vision). The new IKON reached out to include men when it made sense to do so: for example in its Art Against Apartheid issue, a compendium of work by U.S. and South African writers published in the United States before the ANC came to power, and which has long since become a collector's item.

Susan's contribution to a deep understanding of the interplay between poetry and politics goes far beyond her work with IKON. It is most brilliantly expressed in her own poems. In the brief preface to *With Anger / With Love: Selections: Poems & Prose (1963-1972)*, she writes:

> *In a poem, words are used to achieve an understanding that can only be grasped by the combinations of the words, by their sound, their music, mirroring the full unity of language, the emotion and thought of the poet, the style of the poet's life.*
>
> *[…] The demands of revolution have always been the demands of art […] The creative process, a process which is capable of moving us to ever higher levels of comprehension can take place only from a perspective that speaks from experience rather than rhetoric, that speaks from the core of human involvement rather than from the periphery.*

In the volume you hold in your hands, so many pieces embody this early understanding. "A Poem that Starts in Winter" does so with lines such as:

This is a poem about digging images from rage   when all else fails
when there is no common past
An anger imbedded so deeply
it survives.

And in the poem titled "Red," we read:

...As a child
my chosen favorite was blue
It still is   But I turn to red
as one turns to the future
As one is pulled by the future
to be acknowledged & met

In "Genesis":

It would be a lie to say that it was over. Any of it.
To say that yesterday, suddenly, it was different.
In a way there is a change. Desire is no longer a path,
no longer a cause, no longer a blindness.
No longer a strength.

As I cite lines and stanzas from Susan's poems, I can hear her reading, her unique voice imbuing them with her thoughtful intonation: the passion and also the silences. In her work often the deepest passion resides precisely in the silences. Hers is an open intonation, straightforward, quiet and then building in intensity, dependent for its resonance on a perfect marriage of heart and mind. Occasionally there is irony, as in these lines from "Facts":

In my class I ask
"What is a fact?"
A student answers
"What you hear on the 5 o'clock news."

There is a commanding, yet vulnerable power. And Susan reads with her whole body, avoiding that arbitrary line break and distractingly imposed staccato characteristic of so many poets of our generation. On the page, within the line itself she often uses slightly longer than usual spaces between words to indicate pauses, so the reader understands exactly how to articulate her phrasing. I find myself wishing this long-awaited anthology came with a CD so readers might be able to hear the work in her voice as well as read it.

Women have always been central to Susan's life, from the mother who chose husband over daughter, to friends and lovers throughout the years. She came out to herself as a lesbian long before it was safe or comfortable to do so publicly. It is impossible today, when so many of us claim our gender identity almost without question, to be able to assess what that meant back then. In *America's Child* she writes about a benefit reading for the Greenwich Village Peace Center in the 1960s, organized by Grace Paley and Robert Nichols, which included among the readers Denise Levertov and Allen Ginsburg:

> *... I would be reading a poem I had written for Norma— without the dedication. [...] [I read the poem and] there was loud applause. I sat down, relieved, happy to be able to relax and enjoy the rest of the reading, when Denise turned to me with a puzzled look and said, "What strange images for a woman to use." To which Ginsberg commented wryly, "That's because she's gay..."*
>
> *A few weeks later when I sent Denise a new batch of poems [...] I got a note back from her that she was disappointed in my work, it seemed to her I was basically always writing about the same subject. She never mentioned what that subject was. I didn't understand.*
>
> *Or maybe I understood only too well.*

That was the end of my contact with Denise until many years later. She would become one of the American poets actively involved in anti-war and political protest. In the Seventies, we read together again, different people in a different world. In 1975, she was responsible for publishing my poem "Amerika," an extremely radical poem, in the American Poetry Review. *But I can only guess what the loss of her patronage during those important early years had meant.*

In the 1960s and for many years thereafter, the Left did not look sympathetically on open expressions of gay love (which many Communist parties and other Left configurations considered deviant). On the other hand, the artists, by and large, remained unconcerned with social change. Susan courageously embraced both worlds, the first as a matter of identity, the second out of belief and conviction. Because commitment runs in her veins, in her writing and in her life, she has long bridged what happens in the world and in the human heart. More often than not, this insistence upon standing exactly where she knows she must has left her very much alone.

One reviewer who praised her memoir (*New York Times Book Review,* Feb. 10, 2008), wrote: "Sherman's subject is finding herself—discovering and accepting her love of women—and learning her art. [Her] account ends in 1970, but for her the experience of the women's and gay liberation movements still lies ahead."

Movements mean community, and although Susan has been at the center of several of her era's key communities, her life and work have also prefigured them to some extent. The question, with regard to the work, is whether in Susan's life the time between taking a stand and finding a supportive community created a vacuum. In a vacuum several things can happen: momentum may be lost, but the visionary may also create her finest work. Loneliness is also inevitable.

Men have also been important in Susan's life. There was Allen Katzman, who was part of the world that became the alternative to the suffocation of her parents' home. There was Theodore Enslin, the New England poet whose friendship spans many years; other male poets of her generation such as Robert Nichols and Jerome Rothenberg. And there is the legendary but very real figure of Cuban revolutionary commander René Vallejo Ortíz, Fidel Castro's personal physician, who invited her to Cuba when she was ill and could not afford proper medical attention in New York. The poems to him in this book are many-layered.

Courage, then, has been a central thread in Susan's life and work. Not the easy courage of broad ideas and self-evident social truths, but the much more nuanced and difficult courage that carries so many of her poems to that high mountain ridge where earth falls away at sharp angles on either side and a delicate pathway barely sustains the feet.

She explores love through its loss or absence, life through an awareness of death, times and events and people through gestures so tenuous they are all but imperceptible before she gets us to sit up and take note, listen, look, feel. Take, as examples, these lines from "Areas of Silence":

> *It is not of death I am afraid, but the moment before death. It is not action that makes me afraid, but consciousness*

or from "Here's a Poem," a tribute to poetry and the poets who write it, particularly those who are unknown and unnamed:

> *Here's to all that magic music beauty*
> *surprise that died unsung   that dies everyday*
> *The blood that moves us forward*
> *that holds back the tide*

or from "Second Thoughts":

It is not true no one ever dies
of love. It's the only thing anyone
ever dies of   seeing the last remnants
of their life   what they hang on to
what ties us to this earth
drifting away

or from "Morning Poem":

I am inside
                    and outside
of it all
I reach out
with what is behind me
I live my death
                    am captured
in my life

I have often pondered the ingredients that produce this sort of sensibility and mind. Born in Philadelphia, Susan grew up in the Hollywood of the 1940s. Her parents were divorced when she was four, and her stepfather was an actors' agent for Abbott and Costello among other stars of the era. Her mother, from a Jewish immigrant family, left her working class husband to find her identity in the ephemeral trappings of that world: the furs and rings, the status. When her daughter finally left home, drawn by the lore of a life of creativity, repelled by her stepfather's abuse, her mother sided with her husband's insanity, offered Susan $50 and told her to leave. Seventeen years later the poet would return to say goodbye to the woman who had given her life. Susan has never known her maternal grandparents' names, has only in recent years discovered those of her paternal grandparents. Hers was an upbringing in which the erasure of history was cultivated, memory discouraged, awkward or uncomfortable ties cut, and new beginnings sought for class and status salvation. Pretend or imagine into existence the life you want or need.

And so Susan was forced out and away. And she embarked on her own necessary journey, one deeply influenced by her parents' choices but also radically different. Where she had experienced abuse, she searched for loyalty and nurturance. Where she had known silence, she discovered her voice. Susan's work seeks to understand the cultural and economic forces that shaped her parents' lives as well as her own. She references the warmth and delight in certain childhood moments as well as, more obliquely, those crimes committed against her capacity for self-confidence, trust, and possibility.

In other words, like so many of our generation she escaped. But we never entirely escape our earliest scenarios and demons, habits and expectations. Susan studied at Berkeley, came of age in the turbulent movement-energized days of that northern California city during the San Francisco Renaissance and the House Un-American Activities Committee (HUAC)'s west coast hearings and the "police riots" they provoked. She encountered poetry and politics—creativity and change—at one and the same time, and they remain inextricably linked in her experience. When she made her own version of going "on the road," and moved to New York in 1961, she was following an eastward trend that would explode in the early coffeehouse readings, the new publications, Civil Rights, protest against the American war in Vietnam, happenings and experimental theater.

Several of the poems in this collection offer portraits of New York as sharp as any I've read. For example, a poem called "Holding Together" which evokes, for me, a woman's version of Ginsberg's "Supermarket in California":

If you look for me
in the supermarket on Avenue A
on a Saturday morning

> *among green beans*
> *and bananas   rhododendrons*
> *snake plants   Swedish ivy*
> *small cans of tuna salmon spam*
> *Do not expect to find me…*

But the world didn't end for Susan at 14th Street, as it did for so many downtown city dwellers of those years. She traveled to Cuba (we spent time there together, at the Cultural Congress of Havana in January, 1968) and would later spend several life-changing months on that island. She visited Chile during the Popular Unity government and Nicaragua during the heady Sandinista years. And she spent time in Spain and Mexico, the former reflected in her exquisite "Barcelona Journal," the second surely background for her suite of poems to Sor Juana Inés de la Cruz, the 17th century nun who many believe to be the greatest woman poet of the Spanish language. This suite is a conversation between women linked across centuries by intellectual curiosity, desire and literary brilliance. Time collapses beneath the power of its intuitive magic. It is one of the high points in the collection.

The Sor Juana poems are accompanied by the photographs of Joséphine Sacabo. There is an exciting and fortuitous relationship between Susan's poems and Joséphine Sacabo's art: photographic images that have been worked and reworked so that they "take place" on several levels. The figures (often female) who emerge from the extraordinary texture in a number of the prints seem to echo Sherman's own reach for deeper meaning beneath the surface of each word, each line. Those accompanying the Sor Juana poems could not do so more evocatively; it is as if both artists were responding to the same powerful pull of this 17th century woman's yearning. This is a happy and meaningful collaboration

And then there are "Areas of Silence" and "A Poem That Starts In Winter"; quite simply among the great poems of the language.

There are poets who spend much of their time promoting their own work, and those who put their energy into publishing the work of others. One of the reasons Susan's poetry is not better known, despite several books and inclusion in many magazines and anthologies, is surely because she herself has not put the same effort into marketing it as she has put into producing and publicizing the work of others, however worthwhile an effort that might be. I am not only referencing self-interest here; personal history and temperament also lead a person in one direction or another. Self-promotion requires self-interest, and this was knocked out of Susan early on.

Susan Sherman's poetry gives us World in all its subtlety, complexity and wonder; intimacy in all its truth; contradiction in its potential for revealing the human psyche; and unwavering commitment. Read these poems, absorb them at both the conscious and unconscious levels, and then read them again. I guarantee you will discover something new and useful each time: heartbreaking and energizing at one and the same time.

—Margaret Randall
Summer 2011

Genesis

A POEM THAT STARTS IN WINTER

This is a poem for people without a history
whatever their color   whatever their race
who can't remember their mother ever holding them
talking to them about their past
Who find themselves in unknown places
without instructions   & without a guide

This is a poem for the children of immigrants
whose parents wanted so much to forget   to leave behind
the places they were born   the places they fled
they never spoke of those days to their children
never even told them their grandparents' names
Who died leaving their children lost   and restless
rootless   hungry

This is a poem that starts in winter
but never ends   A poem about people
about individuals   with specific features
Proper names

This is a poem for Sarah whose mother was Jewish   but no one could tell
She had blond hair blue eyes   It was 1939
She taught Sarah a lesson about vision
how to make people see past you   how to hide
In moments of doubt they would always throw it in your face
You could count on it
"Dirty Jew"

This is a poem about words

This is a poem about Sarah's mother
Who never stepped inside a synagogue after the age of eight

Who never forgave her own parents for what she was born
an immigrant   poor
Who lived her contradictions until the day she died
Who left her lie behind her   A legacy drawn
in her daughter's face

This is a poem for Sarah's mother   A poem about words

This is a poem for Barbara   1961   Whose father warned her
if she were involved with those radicals at Berkeley   those "Reds"
he would be the first to give her name to the FBI   to turn her in
She never doubted he was serious   She learned that day never to trust
& never to speak

This is a poem about trust

This is a poem for Carole who cried out in shame
discovering her ancestors had killed & robbed
to gain a country   Carole who had a history
She no longer wished to claim

This is a poem for a Vietnamese poet   Havana, 1969
who praised three young Americans for their courage
standing against their own country   their own people
for what they felt right
He had no choice   was forced to fight   No virtue in that
They thought him too generous   mistaken at best
But still it helped   But still it healed

It was winter then too

This is a poem about digging images from rage
when all else fails   when there is no common past
An anger imbedded so deeply
it survives

This is a poem about war

This is a poem for Brenda   who fell in love with a woman
years before it became a political act
Who decades later still stumbles over words long forbidden
jealous of those who proclaim their love nonchalantly
"Lesbian"

This is a poem for Brenda
This is a poem about words
A poem about winter   A poem about war

This is a poem for those caught between worlds
squeezed between times   for people without a history
who connect with no ancestral past

This is a poem about them   about me

This is a poem about words like dialogue compassion
which have yet to appear   but people this poem
About war contradiction rage choice anger
trust

This is a poem that starts in winter
but never ends

This is a poem about people   individuals
with specific features
Proper names

DEFINITIONS

1

I think it's coming close to death
that does it
        both others
      & your own
that magnifies the values
begins the definitions

This morning
        mild at last
      after weeks of chill
Streets heavy with water
People stepping
            cautiously
      hardly know where
      to place their feet
so accustomed to barriers
                of salt and ice

My mind resembles those winter streets
gray
    with sludge
The snow cover melted
The sidewalks washed of unfamiliar
glare

2

After all   she said
What difference does it make?
That's the reason I never write
hardly speak   of what is me

I began to answer glibly   stopped
Held myself in identical fear
My own touch tentative
                    almost an excuse
like making love to someone
for the first time
or the third (which is always harder)
once you begin to know   experience
another
        The tension of your hair   brown
        streaked with gray
                    The lines of
        your face   like wires   rushing through
        my hands   the pressures of your past
        your forehead   your knees

3

Warm outside   the steam
continues   forced by habit
I open the window   throw the
oracle   trace the heat
The heart thinks constantly it says
One constant then the heart   another
the drawing back
                Four o'clock
two hours till dawn   Nightmare
image   your face
surrounded by strangers
Beloved   you turn
                    away

4

Death brings us close to it
Death itself

        forgetting
And we the living
wanting to remember
not wishing to be forgotten
                  separated
from what we hold most near

I hold you for a moment   lose you
watch you disappear
            I hold you
for a lifetime   lose you

the next year   the next morning
the next minute   the next breath

5

You tell me
What can I say to that young woman
eighteen years of age?

That I at thirty-eight must once more lay aside
all sense of definition   order
Must once more carefully measure
the accumulation of my years

Or should I say
her question can be answered
in specific needs   others
and her own
        But she's asking
more than that We both know
what she means

The only real difference being death
The one who stops the heart

THERE WAS A WOMAN ONCE

who was more to me than words   any blending
of alphabet and sound   We met at the corners of day
in the space where night crosses light
where shadows fold into darkness
The moments between our meetings
were air   Twenty years lie between her
and this poem   a length of time
impossible to render

There was a woman once who was more
to me than imagination   wonder
the chimeras that embrace the night
More than the chill kiss of wind that tortured
her secret into patterns of light and
breeze   A woman who was more to me than
forever   the bending of syllable and time

We met on a hilltop in Vermont   made love
in the sweetgrass of our desire
These are moments that defy forgetting
These are moments time cannot cure with
detail noise distraction   Mornings that bound us
sticky and tight   with dew

There was a woman once who was more to
me than flesh   We touched to open
and then once again to close
the way a negative is held over wary eyes
to keep the sun from blinding in the madness
of its fire   What lay between us was that
strong   What joined us was that fierce
Lying in each other's arms

Married   she had never meant for us to happen
had seen me as diversion   a momentary lapse
Now she called me treasure   promised
to keep me always   cherished
hidden   in her private place
But forever is a length of time like any other

One afternoon   precisely at the stroke of one
she lapsed into a silence without boundary
The air lay like a tomb around us
She could not look at me   touch me   say my name
She had never meant it to go so far
It had become too much for her to bear
This woman who meant more to me
than words

Should I be grateful   thank whatever gods
or goddesses   gifted me this passion   this legacy
I cannot relinquish   cast aside
Forever is a length of time without forgiveness
After twenty years   I search for her no longer
but for that moment   between opening and
distance   when I held her close
Not yet knowing enough to turn away

HOW A FACE CHANGES

passing from strangeness into something
familiar
The features themselves
                                    changing
          becoming somehow
                different

I thought : the sun   hot   the air
clear   pleasant
                allowing space
                                    breath

                                        a place

I thought : what is missing is something
familiar   the face of a person passing
from strangeness
                        into that other place

Our world is edged by the familiar
is shaped by what is close
How a face changes   What that means

Your face has changed for me
as you become slowly   one of those people
who border the edges
of my days

DURATION

Many nights I waited   Many years
The words slow in coming   Often I called
There was seldom an answer   The magic
beneath my feet   at my fingers   Often I dreamed
To find truth different from the dream

Many nights I waited   Many years   Until the words came
Their form like the earth   Beautiful in their face
To understand is to know in just what way I
walked   The dream that drove me forward
That rests with me still

My friend   As I reach to touch you   So still you are
So near   There is a truth a mirror cannot tell
To understand the dream   To hold it close
As hands   As eyes

When it is so cold the fingers grow chill
When there is no speech because the stillness
must not be broken   When even poems must cease

If I could give you anything   I would give you
this dream   In its contradiction   In its truth
How in action it changes   What in action
it means   How the earth opens her body   Almost
as an act of grace

THE REAL QUESTIONS

Where do you go when there is nowhere
to go   Hesitancy   The inability to act
against   Even if I   The word   The sun
barely   but rising   but rising   pressing further
further   until there is no   And how
so much I want

The eyes open   The hands unfold   The feet begin
to move   Rivers and streams cross   Trees
And in the sky   Heat   Holding this earth to my
lips   Covering my eyes with its cool clean hands
Suspended   Drained   In love with the earth
In love with the smallest things that grow

You go to the north   I to the east   This green land
that pulls us into its arms   As one person we
know   As it pulls us steadily in its own
direction   And in returning   we cross   we move
And in returning we move   As it pulls up deeper
and deeper into itself

Above my head   the depths   the darkness   Below my
feet   the darkness the death   Above my head   Under
my feet   To open is to drop   It is a madness
that they dare to grow

In the way the hands play   In the way the face
gestures   The eyes drawn back   In the
attitude   In the contours   Where do you go
when there is nowhere to go   The fingers loosen
There is this thing that must be touched   One arm

reaching forward   In love with the earth
The sun   To open is to drop   It is a madness
a madness that they dare to grow

RED

Red means STOP
It is the color of fire
of passion   revolution
of the sun rising and setting
It is the color of the heart
Flowers are red   & the devil
It is the color of contradiction
of motion   As a child
my chosen favorite was blue
It still is   But I turn to red
as one turns to the future
As one is pulled by the future
to be acknowledged   & met

GENESIS

1

Night—an interim, a point in time. Along this line, straight,
geometrical, existing only in length, in one dimension,
my memories exist.

All nights placed together. A wall—long, high, without depth.
A slide, curved in space. A steel soldier jerking its arms mechanically
against a small steel drum.

Never remembering after that one day. Red. Blue.
And the sound of the drum, over and over.

My mouth, blind, twists into shapes that have no meaning.
Watching the snow. Listening to ice split against the window.

The stuttering increases.

It is my world, but it is their world too.

2

"I hate you and as long as I'm alive I'll fight you."

Hands shaking. My body exists only as a fist.

"I hate you and as long as I hate you I can live."

The walls move. The face smiles. The voices disappear. The chair,
large, slides over me. My hands become old, wrinkled. I lie on my
back staring at the wall.

"I hate you."

The bed is wood and I am wood. The door shrinks.
I reach over, take it in my hands, stare at its ugliness.

The door becomes large and sharp. I toss it across
the room. The teeth smile. The door smiles.
The ugliness smiles.

The room is squares and cubes and triangles. The
colors, blinding, form into patterns. The rocking begins.

Lines fall apart, curve, ropes, twisting, unbearable.

The movement stops. The room is a room. God disappears
back into the picture frame.

3

The dreams, always of departure. Words jerked from a page—
not even the letters discernible.

Seeing from a distance the space and outline of events.
Sitting in a chair by the piano, pressing the keys down, slowly,
I watch the notes rise above my eyes like people
moving in front of me, speaking.

To move without thought. To move without sight.
To act. The dreams, from a distance, like the ocean moving back
and forth, never touching the sand except in that small margin
of mud and tide.

Lost in images, I walk the borders of days. Words weld together,
indistinguishable from the sound of my mind weaving pictures,
ideas, memories. The refuse is thrown off; the verb disappears;
the adjectives change.

Everything—just to keep order. Just to preserve
stability among the flashes, the arrows of stimuli that vibrate
through my spine. How the baby cries, unable to find an outline
among the shapes that threaten it. How the consciousness groans,
forced to define paths, force directions, dictate systems.

And for one instant, when the process stops. Lost in a blur of color,
sound, echoes, words, voices, motion.

The poem is a poem of endurance.

4

Perhaps the act away from pain is the only true act.

It is hard to forget those nights. It is always harder
at night, curtained from distraction, when the body becomes
its own direction.

It would be a lie to say that it was over. Any of it.
To say that yesterday, suddenly, it was different.
In a way there is a change. Desire is no longer a path,
no longer a cause, no longer a blindness.
No longer a strength.

The strength must lie in a different direction.

Different events. Different people. It would be easier
to give each person speech, to mold each body into words
that are its own. But for what reason?

The voices are all mine. By using my own voice,
even for thoughts not mine, I gain distance.

5

The wind is heavy. At lunch, I walked to the river.
At first it was blocked by cars and then I saw a bridge
and walked across it. The water was black. Choppy.
It became impossible to reconcile the water and the people
walking near me. Once one achieves a distance it becomes hard
to return and harder to explain. It must be done slowly.
Not in a single word, not in a group of words, but in that shapeless
form that measures the space of the water, the sidewalk, the attempt.

You see, even now, I am guilty of thinking that beyond the river,
beyond the sidewalk, there exists something I can describe,
touch, give.

But as I write, the words themselves dissolve
into a distance.

6

Voices. Stretched across mirrors, hitting the glass with
my fists. Not writing because the most secret moments
must be that, secret. The feeling is cruel, alone, the rain pounding
the windows into mirrors. Cruel. That even in those moments
you are not alone.

Opening the window, I reach out, no longer able to think
about the past. The moment itself, once written, past.
The moment itself, once written, the end of all that's
past or now.

A strange noise. The fear in a strange noise,
as if your world could break and suddenly be something different.
Something unreal. Something terrifying.

The world gets between people, pushes them, like leaves or newspaper. Love is an isolate thing. A thing of memory.

Outside fists stretch across the rain. Not written.
Not wishing to be written. Like a cat, always on you, heavy, regardless of its grace. Pushing things over. Breaking them. Clumsy. Indifferent. Like the sirens, the bells of the church. The cat always there. The rain, hot, humid. The disgust knowing that even an empty shell shrieks as it breaks, that none of us are different in our pain, that there is nothing that equals the fragments of a shell scattered like the rain.

When will it stop? So afraid of the ending that words, voices, the cat, anything, even fragments, even the world that comes between us is better.

7

It comes too slowly. The room, loose, wrinkled, like old skin. Comfortable. Even the night, protective. Every thought negated. Not forming a paradox, but an alternative. Not wanting to say exactly what it is I feel, even to myself. As if the saying would erase the negation, reject the alternative.

There was that one day. Alone. No longer myself. No longer in the universe of alternatives. That one day. The coldness of it.

We can only lose the things we love. To enter something apart from words—to find new areas of relationship that are more than different names.

It comes too slowly. Need breaks the room. The fight relaxing into a world that shapes its own images. It is too hard to give up the pleasure of needing things.

8

To know. The beginning always continues. The hours spent in preparation, and always there, again and again, the same. I break your form with a hundred details and always my pencil traces the profile of your voice. Your laughter.

What can I say against your laughter?

So precise. That it should be so precise, my love, that to know it is to know everything.

Years before, the pain. And now, a line, circling into a hand, pointing into space.

Areas of Silence

WHAT I WANT

I want to be free of all the things that
encumber me   of rent & bills   of tomorrow's
breakfast   of yesterday's words
of my fantasies of love   my insatiable
need for love
I want to be free of the knowledge
of things   of my own shape   my structure
of "that's just not the way it's done"
or "if only you'd done it differently"
I want to be free of time   its endless
repetitions   of myself   my name
names   labels   what defines me
I want to be free of others   of their
distinctions   of my need for them
of this poem   words
I want to be free of newspaper headlines
the radio   television   all these things
that encumber me
Please for a moment relieve me of
constant discovery   this prison
perception   But I am grounded in myself
this world I was born to   my passion
for change   to change things
the need to touch   hold   be touched
held

FIRST AND LAST POEMS

for Violeta Parra

there is nothing romantic
about death   about pain
tears falling like soft clouds
like copper clouds   the color of rusted blood
the texture of fire

the first enemy is fear
the second power
the third   old age

all my life   all those books   all those feelings
words   thoughts   experiences
to say such simple words   to feel
such simple things

your mountains   like my own   like home
rows of dust   of light brown soil
as if a gentle wind could level them
could blow them away

the sea   touching my nostrils
filling them   a country of smell
of sound   of wine   flowers   of salt air
of early morning   opening and
opening   through my mind
my heart   the extremities
of my hands   my feet

if I were a bird and could float
dipping and weaving tapestries of air
and light   if we could fly together

like silver crows   birds of dream
until everything stops   is silent and
gentle   like your songs   your voice

but the world allows us nothing
the world is nerves   is fiber
dust and sand   the world changes constantly
nothing remains the same

I see you singing into the air
as if your voice could fly   be free
were there creatures above you
listening   fishing your gifts
from the breeze   was there a place
that could hold you   as you opened yourself
to it   as you went where no one else
could follow   where no one else   could see

> *each time I have loved*
> *I have left part of myself behind*
> *until now I am mostly memory*
> *mostly dream   what I have left*
> *I give to you   my last love*
> *my last song*
>
> *the total of all*
> *I have ever felt or known*

we grow smaller as we grow
as things empty themselves of us
and we   of them

it is so deep   this thing between us
no name can contain it
even time trembles
at its touch

THE MEETING

1

To touch your face
To touch your arms
To touch your waist
To touch your thighs

To touch your sex

To hold it soft against my check
To breathe it slow against my lips
To hold you close against my breast

My love

2

Old as the woman moaning songs
from her chill staccato walls
Old as that   The touch between us
The chant filtering through coarse
night sounds   The touch between us

Can I name you   The words that lie against
me   Soft against the night   Can I call you
The night itself close upon my thighs

To hold you near
To touch your lips
To hold you close as my own breath

3

Touched so deeply that tears come
unnoticed   And without pain   That once
were central   And only pain

It is here between us   Not ourselves
But what is here   In this space

Touched so deeply that love comes
unnoticed   And without pain   That once
was central   And only pain

4

Rain glides in two dimensions   The window
holding it to my face   As I hold you   As I
place my knuckles to your forehead   Moving from
my touch

The vision   two dimensions   The surface
rigid   As we reach toward it   To find it
different   But still there   cool   under
our touch

5

I would hold you gently
Throw myself against you as
the rain   Talk to you of

small things   As you would
touch a child   Or yourself
small and vulnerable to even
the slightest breath

6

No longer afraid   The touch of you deeper
than any fear   Deeper than your naked form
The single syllable of your name

As I touch your body
As I touch the earth
As I touch this paper
As I touch each word

It is everywhere   This night and the
outline of our form   As we are together
Without boundary   Without dimension

As I touch the depth of you
My love

A POEM

For you alone
built word upon word
    like years
like time people share
           together
    deepening
growing into meaning
        word
    upon word
          meaning
    upon meaning
for you alone   a poem

I know your need for form
For things to be
        concrete
the way grass moves & light
the borders
    of your shoes
        the mountains
    of your home
all these things
a kind of boundary
a definition
    a name

if I could offer you the salt taste
of the sea
    if I could turn your home
into a glance
    a gesture
        of the eyes

if I could look at you as home
speak to you as sea

there is nothing on this earth
that does not change
that does not deepen or drift
away

there is nothing on this earth
more concrete
                  than this feeling
        I have
                  now
for you

nothing
is more
        real

A QUIET POEM

Sitting here   alone   reading poems
you have written to others   brief fragments of love
delivered to other ears   I wish I could be
young for you forever   yet retain
the experience of years   the ripening of love
A garden weeded by time   by memory
remembrance of joy as well as pain

This is a quiet poem   this poem I write
for you today   sitting here alone
Sea deep in passion   the ocean we never see
Dark water at bottom of tides and light
held by sand and rock   churning silent
beneath white-tipped waves

In your absence   left with simple words
inadequate metaphors similes   what can I say
Sleep well   my dearest one   sleep well
May night hold you in her arms   and rock you
gently   into dream

A PICTURE PERFECT DAY

Fall leaves beginning to turn   Green fading
into red and brown   The sun   hot
last vestige of summer   No one wants to go inside
Couples clutch the warmth   each other
as if willing time to stop   I feel it too
light sinking into skin   day turning toward night
It will be weeks before we walk together again
Even my home seems empty now
devoid of comfort   I want time to speed up
fast forward   This extravagant fall afternoon
so much like summer   holds nothing without you
is just like any other   Just one more
picture perfect day

LOVE POEM / FOR A CAPRICORN

With a hole in my stomach with four grey hairs with
    a callous on my toe with too many years with too many years
With a record player 53 albums desks and drawers and
    shelves of books rooms of thought I come to you
I come as water I come as rain as light falling great
    distances I come to you
I come to you in sleep as you walk as time
As tides form as illusion I come to you as night as sea
    I come to you with death inside me with the pain of
        death inside me with what it means to leave
I come to you with nothing blind mute I come to you
As laughter I come to you as myself as hair hands eyes
    sex I come to you
In madness in love I come to you in minutes hours seconds
    in walking running swimming crawling flying
With a dirty apartment I come to you with an empty
    refrigerator with a house full of cats
I come to you as water comes to earth as the sea reaches
    toward the sand
As lover as friend I come to you as necessity as need

THERE IS SOMETHING CALLED LONGING

so fragile   it must never be spoken
The wind leaves its mark with invisible palms
The face of the wind is silence
But all this is a facade for something
so simple it defies definition
The world is terrible   huge   beyond
our control   As babies we knew it
As adults we had to pretend to
forget   Longing is part of remembering
and so we declare independence
think we have got it beat   think it
no longer matters
Yet we must fight the distance
with what sustenance   but each other

A FARE/WELL PRESENT

Well   good-bye
and all that means
if in fact it means
anything
          words sometimes
taking the place
of meaning
              like last night
twisted in my own
syllables   trying
to explain

Or that summer
seven years old
first time away from home
A feeling of the heart
but literally that
                  The camp director
calling it "homesick"
or "missing"
Not only that something
was missing
                that I was missing
someplace or someone
but that somehow
I was also missing
from something   somewhere
I wanted to be

A seven-year-old pride
denied it   denies it still

but now with how much more vehemence
command of language
skill with words
                        no longer only
(shoulders out   chest squared)
"homesick   not *me*"
but paragraphs of explanation
reams of words
                        to say only
somewhere something
has been left out
is out of place

And so   as a farewell present
I give you this poem
This feeling of the heart
That when I think of you
leaving
            And when I think of you here
and can't be with you
Even when we are together
when I feel you growing distant
I experience that
                        "missing"
that something
left out
as if I am discovering the word again
for the first time
What it really means

As with all things that move us
deeply
            the feeling comes
                                    first
the experience

As we perceive the meaning
The word
            follows later
"missing"

that space which is not empty
but fills all space

AREAS OF SILENCE

1

To startle the past into order. To break the miles.

If it is possible to talk about people, it is possible to talk about love. If it is possible to talk about the city, warm under the rain, it is possible to talk about love.

Words are no more than the objects they represent. To touch them the way one touches plaster, the window glass, the stickiness of a moist, humid afternoon. Knowing it is not that anything is forbidden, but that the past does not easily shape itself into form.

The sound of your voice is the sound of my fingers trying to construct images. As if each word must be physically molded, formed, shaped into existence. Formed. And then forgotten.

To recognize everything must be written. That even the introduction is essential.

That even without us, the sidewalk defines the same pattern.

2

The street is bare is the rain. Quiet. Music from the apartment house filters unevenly through the mist. Everything seems to be just behind me as I walk. The music. The sound of people talking, arguing, singing. The present becomes as distant as the faintness of concrete walls and odors mingle with the salt of your own flesh.

It is difficult to retain the freshness of experience if one is not willing to face the strangeness and horror of it. To believe it as it is. To accept, not the past, but the footsteps that create it.

A drunk slips to the sidewalk. He lies there, the rain bouncing against his arm. I stand for a moment, looking at him.

The sidewalks dissolve. Not a path stretching endlessly to no certain point, but no path at all. To try only to avoid facility, to relate without judgment. No. To allow the possibility of anything. Even of facility. Even of judgment. To allow each unit of experience to build its own set of existences. To start from any point in any universe. To start with a drunk stretched across the rain.

3

Years. To be able to see what it was that linked us, binding us together as irrevocably as that boat carried me from the city, from the details of your face, your body, your words.

I trace my memories with your form and because you are no longer a part of my body, no longer anything except the part of me which can reach through distance, I can define the present.

Knowing memory binds one to the present.

You made the mistake of thinking by arousing feeling in me, my feeling would be directed toward you. As if you could control my past, my blood, my memories. As if these things were yours to control.

The boat moves forward, unaware of the distances it forces to the pattern of its motion.

If you could believe the roles could have been enacted by anyone. It was inevitable that the events should have somehow been created.

I rub my finger across the rain, touch my hair, wishing it were yours. Trying to center you in the city, catch you in the square of its sidewalks. Knowing even then it would take more distance than water.

It is not that the ocean acts as a boundary or even a space,
but that the smallest parts of it somehow separate us from ourselves.
As if the water could recognize us and in that recognition we could
lose the parts of ourselves described as unique.

Turning, I watch the land grow smaller, moving backward,
shrinking into itself. I watch the foam break, white, against the edge
of the boat. The smell of the water, the wind, tight against
the corners of my face.

We are one person now. One action. One voice.

Where is the measure that can separate us?

4

How strange—hearing from you. After so long. I think of myself,
of how much I must have changed. Of how inaccurate my picture
of you, as you exist now, must be. You write me the details
of your life. They mean nothing to me. The people you mention
I do not know. The people I know do not exist for you. I wonder
sometimes what it was I loved—how many people went into
the conception I loved as you. I suppose that more than anything
else I wanted something to give meaning to my life. I wanted that
one thing to be a single person. And unable to find what I wanted,
I created it.

5

In early evening when color seems to stand apart from the objects
which hold it, I sometimes walk along the edge of the pavement,
and staring into the faces of people who pass me, see your face.

Remembering how we walked through empty mornings.
The only interruption the sound of an occasional bus. The crisp
silence breaking the sidewalks into a path for our feet only.

It is only in those moments I remember it was through you
I discovered my own hands, my own eyes, my own flesh.

We move toward each other, merge, move away, move toward
another shape—different only because of the path of our motion.
If I never saw you as you see yourself. If I must create you now,
years later, say if you can I cannot understand the world
you felt once, feel now.

If somewhere, in some universe, you still exist.

6

To want something beautiful so much you are willing to give up
everything to create it. And then to find it is something
you cannot touch.

To want to feel your own body so much, you realize it is made up
of more than the number of bodies that have known it,
that it has known.

Until whatever it is that calls itself by our name goes its own way,
scarcely caring whether we follow or not.

The city leans toward me. Watching the people. Watching the rain.
It breaks. Folds. I see you in front of me, your hands moving in
circles, separating the space around you. The miles I walk on the
moist pavement. As if by walking, I could become part of your
hands, your space.

I turn. Leave the drunk behind me, lying, face down,
on the sidewalk. The rain has stopped and people crowd
into the street. I move against the dampness of my clothes,
voices surrounding me like the hollow sound of the rain.

7

So much length. And the hunger. The afternoon, hot, crawls through
the room. So many faces. And the hunger. A record spins and spins
and spins and somewhere a child lies against a distance
of broken afternoons.

I think sometimes there must be more than this: the words, the heat,
the distance of memory. But then in action, so strange, and always
the hunger and always the dreams.

Ahead the walls expand. My hand reaches to their distance.
But always they move. Further. Further. My mind cannot grasp
their immeasurable distance.

*If it were possible to break your motion with my hands I would do it.
I talk to you, knowing you are not listening to me. Even as I talk, my
words become yours, my face becomes yours. When I finish, I will no
longer exist except as part of you. Do you think it is easy for me? Do you
think my hands are the whole of it, that the way they move defines my
motion? If I could I would kill you as you stand there destroying me
with my words. If I could I would kill you. If only to convince you of
my existence apart from you.*

The walls expand. I can no longer hold their space.

8

Treading the night between my heels. Each step, a step of which
I am unaware. Later, I mark the length of each footprint, of each
block. Of each city. But now, as I walk, I walk without logic.
Without instinct.

A dog lies asleep in the dirt. His muzzle buried deep in the rich,
brown dust. He scarcely breathes. Thin, he seems to have grown there,
to have sprung up suddenly and quietly, like some strange plant.

My steps sound too lonely in the street. My name forcing me into a unity which mocks me. With names, a story of lines, of spaces, of intervals. The miles I walk. The fragments I hide.

But sometimes, you see, I just don't care. Riding a bus. Watching people move around me. Fat, with years of starch, with years of work. Poor, with years of feeding children into a city alien to even the inflection of their speech. Sometimes I share their fat, their dislocation. Sometimes I laugh through their eyes, bend with their muscles. Free of the past and the names that define me.

To travel so fast there can be nothing but this. To speed past the arguments, the reasons, the attempts at unity. The attempt to find a point at which each point is definable.

My steps sound too lonely. My footprints forcing me into a space, a way of speech. Knowing the arguments, the reasons, the compensations, the rewards, the desire. Knowing the desire.

But sometimes I touch my own flesh. And only that it is my flesh. And only that it is soft to my touch.

Sometimes, you see, I just don't care.

9

Words—no more than the outer edge of silence.

What have we left to say, you and I. The dozens of us crowded into a single space, a parallel moment. The words. Written. Spoken. The time etched between each syllable.

That is part of it. But only a part.

The cold creeps around the edges of my shoulder. Listening. Thinking. At this moment only. And then.

And then?

It is not of death I am afraid, but the moment before death. It is not action that makes me afraid, but consciousness.

What have we to say to each other, more than this?

I hold your hand, feel your pulse against my arm. Caught in a moment of desire, I fall. Backward. Heavy. Thinking that finally here. Here.

There is no escape. There is no turning back.

To move is to be touched. To be flung, lucid, against the inner layers of the rain.

To know is to touch. To be killed by the sun.

The Fourth Wall

HERE'S A POEM

to the poets who die unknown
who live their poems day by day
bare the chaos of lost words
Here's to the poems that never get published
that lie fallow in someone's veins
that burned in Hiroshima and Nagasaki   Vietnam
Here's to the poets in Nicaragua
Mexico   Cuba   South Africa   El Salvador
in the southern countryside of all the Americas
and the northern cities too
Here's to the women and men
who never even knew they were poets
had no one to tell them
didn't know how to tell themselves
Here's to the millions of words buried in a
million places all over the globe
The mouths and hands silenced forever
Here's to all that magic music beauty
surprise that died unsung   that dies everyday
The blood that moves us forward
that holds back the tide

REMINISCENCES

for Cuba

& for *Meg*

1

Speaking to you   I was reminded
of those weeks   how far they seem
distant & yet   how strong

speaking to you

words fail me now   often
I sit for hours   without speech
images stray through my mind   songs

as I work a feeling of hunger   and then
of pain

Sometimes   no often   it is harder to remember   and then
on the faces   I discover it   in the streets as I walk
learning to look out boldly   into those eyes

it is not despair that turns them away   but hope
you asked why   & that is the answer

refusing solace   refusing their dark places
their tombs

I sicken of those eyes   their sharp edges   their
wit   I sicken of the sophistication
of those eyes

by their death   they remind me

as those others did

            that winter

so few weeks ago (we spoke together then)

as they did

        by their life

2

It is the song that has meaning   I heard them
sing   We heard them   in their winter   Their
hands   their voices   the song   as the poem
its words strong

& behind the words   the meaning   the syllables
the depth

There is this pain inside me   For years now
I have known it   This pain   This companion of
mine

It reduces things cleverly this friend

What is greater than I

                        it croons to me
it sings to me

What is greater than I

There are things greater   good   good   good

good   What are they
What is more important than this pain

How cleverly it reduces things   this ache
in my side

& those weeks made it deeper   I know now

what caused it   & that it will never leave

3

It reminded me   your voice   of those days
The sea outside my window   I could never live long
beyond the reach of sea   At least sensing it there
its song   even its silence   Always
I have lived near water   & there   it surrounded me

The East River is not an ocean
Is not beautiful like that sea
Does not break against the streets
furious   & then   calm

But it is water   & every now and then a boat passes
& the stillness of it   even the darkness
sometimes

& I see into it as one looks into water

with the backs of the eye

4

It is not finished   is never over
Repeating again and again   Each time holding
the balance   tipping it
forward
The revolution is for people
they said   but it was not
their words

     it was them

the way they were   the way they spoke

It was as hard to carry as water

And now months later   I have begun to
live   to speak   the change

the words written in blood in pain

You could scream it in the streets
and who would listen

But the scream remains   the sound of it
like the sound of your voice   and those
others   like their memory   like water

changing   as it flows

THE FOURTH WALL

1

From which direction does the wind flow? It flows from the East.
From which direction does the wind flow? It flows from
the East and into my hands.

Analysis. Cross-reference analysis. The age of analysis.
Psychological, philosophical, poetic analysis. Not the event, but
the picturing of the event.

Days, dwarf-like, with tinsel hats. America. Orange. sticky,
matted.

My father was from Russia. When he was a small child, he
crossed the borders of his country with a half-dozen other
refugees. He often spoke of the town in which he was born.
A small town. Long rows of hot, sandy streets. Plain one-story
buildings. The cries of Cossacks cutting through the level dirt
walks of his home.

"Jew," they yelled, and he ran. "Jew," they yelled, and he ran across
a continent. "Jew," they yelled, and he crossed an ocean.

They never really believed they had left for good. They never even
learned to speak the language. But my father learned. When he
was twelve, he learned—my mother waiting for him across the
length of a continent.

How many years does it take? In this, my sweet-smelling land. In
this, my sweet-smelling land, where there is no question of time.

They say a desert is an uncultivated region without inhabitants; a
wilderness. A dry barren region largely treeless and sandy. This is

only partly true. My desert is decorated with pinecones and exotic spice. In spring, the cactus blooms into small, pink flowers. My evenings are colder than it is possible to imagine. I take off my clothes at night so I may lie naked. Next to the warm body of my desert. My beautiful, beautiful desert.

2

This morning I had a dream. But I have already forgotten. "Yama." "Yama." Hanging onto her grandmother's brightly colored skirts. "Watch out for the cars." The rolling cars, with their brightly colored skirts.

That wasn't the way it was, but it was the way it might have been. The roads, long, curved. The roads that curled into the desert. The roads that curled around that patch of land, tying it like a Christmas package with light and warmth and

This morning I had a dream. The bus traveled to the edge of a large, blue lake. Not across roads, but through fields and tall, thin arms of grass.

"Yama," she called, and the call curled around me. "Yama," she called.

Los Angeles is situated in a basin. A flat, grey basin surrounded on four sides by mountains. One of the sides folds down long banks into the sea. Every year or so a part of this fourth wall collapses.

From which direction does the wind flow? It flows from the sea. From which direction does the wind flow? It flows from the sea and into my hands.

San Francisco is water and, crossing the bridge, patterns of lights. Lights suspended on air, on water. And on clear days, rows of hills with houses clutched to their sides. There is a vastness about the land, about the coast. Everything seems too large, unmanageable, like objects to the hands of a small child. The East Coast is different, and New York is cluttered and the distance across the palm of the hand.

Los Angeles, San Francisco, New York. The fourth wall is of an indeterminate size and shape. A desert. An impartial country where the other three are joined together.

Every year or so part of that fourth wall collapses.

3

Clear, the music cries and circles the empty space. Clear and compact like a tightly resolved dance. Like this first afternoon as I wander the streets, as others do, as I see it in their faces also, as I walk. New York. Different as it is now, on this first day of warmth.

Clarity is much to be desired and simplicity is the essence of God. These the words of the Saint. Clarity is much to be desired. Clarity is much... to be...

Whose feet are these that walk along the streets? Whose hands hang down from whose body? These are my feet, my hands, my body. This is my face. The face of the blocks as they pass. In face of the blocks as they pass. In face of these members of my body, my face faces the street. The blocks are passed.

4

They said it was the best our country had to offer. Of itself, with no intrusion. Behold, here is the land. Behold, here is the school. Behold, here is the fist, bulging, its muscles veined with the gold of the earth.

But it was not the earth of which they spoke. It was the blood of the earth, cut from its body. Los Angeles. Gigantic. Now red. Now purple. Now the Virgin Mary on the boulevard, white and yellow light bulbs falling from her lips.

I said I did not understand. They said I was young, it was a matter of growth. Of learning how to wield the sickle, spread the refuse out, side by side, with the long, uneven rows of grass. When the settlers first came it was a barren country—a desert surrounded by deserts. They brought the stucco and concrete. They brought the horses and the children. They rode over vast ranches of cattle and grain.

This, my father, is what I am. Because one day I stumbled and scarred my knee so that now, years later, I can still see the small white dots standing out against my leg. And after that how hard I found it to walk on your streets.

I took a brush. It was red. I took a brush. It was green, orange, yellow. I took a brush. It was the width of the desert. And into this city I was born and first heard my name.

When you are grown your brush will be red—the color of this city. You will live here, work here, be married here, raise your children here. You will die here.

I will not die in this city. I will not be the color of this desert, cut down the middle with blood.

It was raining when I left and raining when I arrived. The streets, the houses, the color of rain. When I was a child I wanted only two things—I wanted to learn and I wanted to write.

This is the way the lesson goes: in that first city there were shapes, huge and grotesque. In the second there was water, and the land like an arm extended to the sea. The third was built on a rock that could not support its own weight. There were people. The people that built the city. And there was the fourth ...

Long rows of tightly corseted women through the wide, flat streets. Nothing in that hot sun that was not bright, not stripped with color. And the eyes. Always the eyes. Dressing, living, speaking, dreaming for the eyes.

My father, my mother, my country. The dream that my country provoked in them, in me. This is what you made me. What I am. You gave me eyes and hair. You gave me a body. You sent me out—not as one person, but as a group of people, living under the same skin, gathered together under this union of eyes, hair, body. You gave me a name and you robbed me of that name. You gave me all these things and robbed me of them. But you could not take from me what was never yours to give.

I will not die in your city. I will not be buried under your streets. I will not dress myself in your houses of gold and lies and grotesque forms.

Always you will live here, close as the blood that flows through the veins of my hand. As I walk into the desert. Father, mother, country. The dream clutched tight to my body, like a lover.

LILITH OF THE WILDWOOD,
OF THE FAIR PLACES

And Lilith left Adam and went to seek her own place
and the gates were closed behind her and her name
was stricken from the Book of Life.

1

And how does one begin again

(Each time, each poem, each line, word, syllable
Each motion of the arms, the legs
a new beginning)

women   women surround me
images of women   their faces
I   who for years   pretended them away
pretended away their names   their faces
myself   what I am   pretended it away

as a name exists to confine to define confine
define   woman   the name   the word   the definition
the meaning beyond the word   the prism   prison
beyond the word

to pretend it away

2

It's the things we feel most
we never say   for fear perhaps
that by saying them   the things we care most
for   will vanish
                    Love is most like that
is the unsaid thing   behind the things we do
when we care most

3

to be an outcast   an outlaw
to stand apart from the law   the words
of the law
        outlaw
           outcast

cast out   cast out by her own will
refusing anything but her own place
a place apart from any other
           her own

I do not have to read her legend in the ancient books
I do not have to read their lies
She is here   inside me
I reach to touch her

my body my breath my life

4

To fear you   is to fear myself
To hate you   is to hate myself
To desire you   is to desire myself
To love you   is to love myself

Lilith of the Wildwood
Lilith of the Fair Places

who eats her own children
who is cursed of god

Mother of us all

A WORD TO THE WISE

You will be tomorrow   what you are today
so spake Krishnamurti   venerated Indian sage
but I'm not convinced   if true I'd still be
one day old   Something has to be added
somewhere   to construct a life

Sitting on the edge of the arroyo
brilliant New Mexican day
                              I try to open up
listen through each pore
The sound of the wind against dry leaves
round   like wooden coins clicking together so gently
they can barely be heard

Let even your mind wander   hold nothing back

I succeed for moments   get cold
go back indoors
                          I used to believe in a river of dream
I could dive into at will   the energy of world
beyond worlds   But even then I had my doubts
I have no ancestors to call out to   no old men
will doven away my fear
                              What is there
in your bag of words   Krishnamurti
for the woman I am   not just
for the creatures of your imagination
who can learn how to say *yes*   and forget

CASUALTIES OF WAR

There are some pictures in the mind
impossible to forget   Over the phone
her words barely perceptible   her voice thin
Susan, I love you   Both knowing
these are the last words that will pass between us   ever
as she slips back into a coma   to die at thirty-five
a breast tumor   undetected   until too late

There are secrets we shared   connected in friendship
struggle   that will never be revealed   and others
The night she appeared at my door   suitcase in hand
crying   stunned   arriving home unexpectedly
to find her boyfriend activist hero
with a needle in his arm   a packet of white powder
balanced on the bathroom shelf

Susan, I love you   I put down the phone
never pick it up again to say her name
With all we went through together   that night
for the first time   I call myself coward
Sonia   we both knew   it was just too much to bear

And now   years later   I sit and watch the death
of another friend   We don't share the same events
have lived different lives   Only one secret
passed between us   AIDS

There is no way to hide that name

This time I sit day by day   watching him slowly
die   Watching the words drift away from his lips
and then his mind   as less and less enters
through closed and hooded lids   This time
it is already too late to turn away

I see now how struggle can drain you   wear you out
in unexpected ways   A war is hardest
when the enemy is undefined   When so few recognize
there is an enemy   a human face   beneath inhuman acts

Make no mistake   this is no elegy   no lament
These people are not victims   martyrs
They are casualties of a war   they struggled
all their life to win

IT WAS EASIER THEN

Everything always seems easier in retrospect
When the stakes are lower
The odds evened out by time

It was easier two decades ago   three
The Sixties Seventies
Easier when we lost the war
(No one likes to be a loser)
Easier to have heroes you could support
Ho Chi Minh   Haydée Santamaria
George Jackson   Fred Hampton Rosa Parks
Lolita Lebrón   Assata Shakur   Martin Luther King
Malcolm X

It was easier to be twenty
The future interminable
The past a history lesson   words on a page
written in script   not blood
Not your own   Not yet

It was easier at thirty   Even at forty
It was easier last year
Yesterday   Ten minutes ago
One second before now

Then is always easier
than *now*

For those who dare look up   out of themselves
past their own eyebrows   the ridges of their nose
the corners of their shoes   They know
the struggle continues   outlasts us all

Now is after all only the continuation of *then*
Tomorrow   the extension of today

Whoever said the journey had an end
Whoever set a time   proscribed a date

FACTS

1

South Africa   September, 1984
A story in the *New York Times*
South Africa
                    40 miles south of Johannesburg
28 dead   600 detained
Picked up at the funerals of their loved ones
and their friends

The photo shows death
                              rebellion
Black people moved again
as they were before
and continue to be
(except in our press)
                    to action
resisting
the lie

Underneath the photo   a caption
No explanation A statement of fact
A lie of omission
"Police Quell a Riot"
as if implying they were doing
a commendable act

So many injured   So many killed
& how many times in our papers
do they tell us

"Why?"

2

In my class I ask
"What is a fact?"
A student answers
"What you hear on the 5 o'clock news."

I laugh but it isn't funny
& I am the only one
who gets the joke

3

"Why!" is not "How!"
is not a recital of physical causes
physical effects
                    It is meaning

The bullet pierced her flesh
because a finger pressed a trigger
& she was in the way
is "how"

Why that gun was there at all
why she was in front of it
why that policeman's finger pressed the trigger

not muscles   but years are behind the answer
not reflexes
                    people

4

October 6—
"Pretoria Will Use Army to End Riots"
"Military called in to support the police"

80 now are dead

October 23—
2 o'clock in the morning
7,000 South African soldiers
(along with police) surround a town
Standing 20 feet apart   guns in hands

Two more townships follow
over 150,000 are interrogated
Their hands are stamped
Their thumbs dipped in orange ink

A general strike is called   succeeds
Now whites also are detained

In Soweto   The people continue to rebel
In Soweto   The people continue to fight back

In Manhattan
My student looks at the 5 o'clock news
His head is filled with facts
He knows nothing   He learns nothing

He doesn't even know *"Why?"*

LETTER FROM HAVANA

for Réne Vallejo Ortiz

1

Always I have found it easier to write in the form of a letter, to imagine I am writing to someone, to have a specific person in mind, a specific idea I am trying to express. To piece together, word by word, a motive, a reaction, a part of my life. As though my hands were that half-way point between my thoughts and my heart.

And so I am writing this letter. Trying to explain a little this one day, or the series of days that make up this letter, this piece of my life. As I begin now, in the month of December, 1968, in the city of Havana, so few and yet so many miles from my home.

2

Home. How many homes. In how many cities. Like the lines of a poem, spreading across a continent and beyond, woven as one, to form one body, one thought. So many places and yet always that one place. Where we are at each precise moment, at each second of time.

It is always hardest to begin. To know where, to know how, to begin. Silent, thoughts flow easily, but now, at this desk, it is hard. There was a time, once, two years ago or more, when time took a different direction. Explaining at the same time so much and yet so little. How it was possible and how I came to be in that place, in the midst of it. Time. Not as we know it, but at another place. As it is. And yet I know now that too was another dream. How much closer and still how far away.

This is not clear. But some things are not said so easily. Are not simple sentences. Are not phrases that come easily to words. Are not of words. But leave behind a level of truth that knows, that feels, that is.

And where is it now? That thing that was felt so deeply. Felt. And then gone. As time passes and we pass with it, leaving behind? A sadness. And a need.

3

We build models mimicking our own form. A camera, a pair of eyes. A tool, an extension of the hand. The connections of our own body. And now our minds…

But that experience. That moment in time. Did it have anything to do with me? What part of me was in it? What was it? what was it I have known—that continues to haunt me, that sets me apart?

(July 10, 12:15 P.M. Philadelphia—a place, a time, a date.)

He read it wrong, so wrong—forgetting, or never having learned, that revolution, revelation was the key. Pluto, patience, the will, the steady and inevitable change.

"We solve today's problems, today."—another voice. This one close, sure, and there too a loneliness beyond death. Beyond my comprehension. Because when others die, that is the pain too great. Pain and knowledge—those two things that set one apart.

Backwards into the future, like passengers on a train, we ride forward, our faces toward the past.

Cancer: water. Libra: the balance. Aries: fire. And always there, like a fist, Aquarius, alone—red, angry, a square of death.

A square of love.

Has it happened before, in other ways, in another time, and I, who am so impatient, waiting, forced now to wait. Because there are things that cannot be pushed.

To prepare, to fight, and to wait.

4

It is another day now. Another of many days. And something new has entered since that time. Because it was not enough to know, because that knowledge must now be transformed, because it is this earth we live on, and apart from ourselves are others who also wait, whose need is greater, because for them not even the first step exists.

It was this I had to learn, that I now know. It was this I learned in a way, last year, one year ago, in this same city, in a way that cannot be erased, that was real, as that other experience also was real. That without those others, nothing exists. Because we do not live   in a world apart. Only our death is ours alone, and that only as experience, not as fact.

Because we die as we live, with those others, or we do not live or die at all.

5

We are condemned to light. And that is the truth of it. And it is now that we begin, together, knowing a certain end. For all of us, together, or for none of us at all.

6

A poem must be written to someone, cannot be created of air, delivered to the wind. And so I write to you, in these sentences, long, broken, whatever it takes to express, but never expresses fully, what it is I must say.

One sentence to say it all. One word. But what is it? Years. And still that cannot be reached.

"We must always remember the complexity of the simple." In a book, somewhere, those words, that ritual, that complex of words, of dance, of song. I fight my own doubt, knowing now, after these years, what is there, fight my own doubt, my eyes, how I see, my hands, how they write, my body, my mind, how it feels, how it sees. Knowing this other, not beyond, but within, as part, all, another way. No longer the pieces. but the whole. Death has many faces. They say a person sees many things before they die, that their life passes before their eyes, that they know what has passed and what is to come.

I thought tonight as I sat, the room turning before my eyes, that I must have died many times. As I saw it turn, my life, before my eyes. I can no longer use the words, must talk to them, must let them talk to me, tell me what they mean.

As they come from other mouths. As I find them on other pages. As I find myself no longer alone.

Havana, Cuba
Winter, 1968

Long Division

MIGRATION

Birds fly south   chained to the wind   They are wild
not free   There is a difference   They move
without reflection   choice   driven by instincts
they cannot begin to understand
What use are words against such need
I thought I could lose my self in wings
but I am held by memory   desire
imagined futures   Citizens of air   of water
earth and sea   we are sisters and brothers
bound together by a destination that calls us
in our blood   But only I can turn around
fly north   change direction   return again
fly south into the wind

SIXTH STREET RHAPSODY

Not a symphony   or the blues   not jazz
an opera aria   There has to be movement
plenty of it   People crossing crisscrossing
sidewalks streets   Twisted ribbons of
sound   Looking for dinner   a clandestine smoke
beer   or just walking   Because it's spring
apartments beginning to swell with
heat   The air already thick   too dense to
breathe   Perhaps a rhapsody is best   something
dramatic   a bit old-fashioned   out of step
out of sync   Apple the mouth says   Where are you
the ear detects   The confusion of not knowing
what to believe   how to act   what to say
Maybe you'd call it blues   a good Nineties version
of a Fifties tune   But there's no magic on earth
that can do that   bring back the past   Get real
it's not spring   It's summer   It's hot
The streets are crowded   It looks like rain

LONG DIVISION

Nothing ever really seems to add up
My mother aged   frail   at seventy-eight
But I don't feel old   Don't feel any different
than I ever did

No different than fifty long years past
before her marriage drained sustained her
with rings and furs   a crazed husband's
unloaded gun pressed against her willing throat

Another piece of meaningless melodrama
in a world where children starve   old people die
lacking a few dollars to pay their bills

She used her talent looks to marry money
tossed her only daughter aside   a complication
An imagined contender for her throne

I could have loved you forever Mom   if you had let me
As it was I left   gave you hardly a backward glance
kept you from becoming my world

only to find the world becoming you

It's not my childhood that betrays me
I've digested that   spit out what I couldn't use
It's a world that's taken on your face
the duplicity of your tongue   your style

Alone at night sensation sinks too deep
In the mind's open cavern language
disappears   Everything is washed away

Even knowing what is real   How righteous anger
saves   Whether I will it or no
Her voice remains

SECOND THOUGHTS

It's not true no one ever dies
of love   Its the only thing anyone
ever dies of   seeing the last remnants
of their life   what they hang on to
what ties us to this earth
drifting away

I think of the painting of four persimmons
A door opening   The virtue
of simple statement

One imperfection is always added
to a work of art   to make it real

After six years we should have
understood   I can't believe we
learned nothing   that those years ground out
only things

I find it hard now to remember
I apply meaning after fact
I forget those small details
that define a life together

What is important is the future
what has the possibility of change
But the past has a place also
is part of it   As my past grows larger
begins to take up the greater portion
of my life

THE PLANTS

I transplanted them
as you suggested
placed new dirt   firmly
around their roots
They are growing well now
as you said they would
leaves   straight out   secure
I remember a story I read once
an Indian parable
how people are like young plants
the care they need
until they are grown
I never had that care   know now
I might never have it
but people   unlike plants
find their own places to root
And what strange flowers
they sometimes grow

AWAKENING

What I miss most in the years since you
have gone is how   as morning rose   you pressed
against me   closed me in your warmth
No matter our distance the night before
angry words   or none at all
sandwiched on both sides by sleep
The tenderness remained

A child I pressed up   against the world
only later learned to shy away
from contact   too sensitive for touch
In youth that changed as words became
worlds   became blows   caresses
A universe colored by fantasy   desire
The softer tones of flesh and dream

These days contact seems ephemeral
eludes me   My world moves more and
more away from simple pleasures
Hands clasped in friendship   or in love
A gentleness that waits

And now sometimes at dawn   half-asleep
a small black kitten circling my knees
pressing against my heart   I reach across my pillow
surprised   to find you missing   Until at last
finally awake   I realize once again
just what it is I crave

IT IS RAINING

                        and quiet
summer over   passing graceless
heavy   from the city
I hear the rain and think
                                of you
your hands   rain   your eyes
rain   the way you speak and walk
rain
        the sound of it
                        the smell
what it brings   what it leaves
behind

If I were somewhere else
if you were there
with me   if we were there
together   if it were a solid space
a place we could lie   talk   think
look at the sky
      touch
if it were raining
                        if we sat there
together   touched there   together
in the rain

I think of rain as green
I think of rain as brown blue
as color without light   as light
without color
      as part of me
barely   like memory   like dream

I think of you as rain
as I see you   in rain
as I wait for you   in rain
as outside summer passes

                   and rain falls

   as it closes me

           lightly

   in its sleep

HOLDING TOGETHER

If you look for me
in the supermarket on Avenue A
on a Saturday morning
      among green beans
and bananas rhododendrons
snake plants Swedish ivy
small cans of tuna salmon spam
Do not expect to find me

Do not expect to find me
in the cafeteria on the corner
eating danish
     sipping coffee
staring at the old men
with their long faces
and tired sleeves

or walking filthy summer streets
greeting a neighbor with short
black hair
     matted dog

If you look hard enough
you may find my footsteps
Indentations on walls
      Faces
my voice has touched
But don't expect to find me
My name scatters itself on
the seasons

I am hidden
even from myself
In that place of solitude where
poems reside
and seams

MORNING POEM

There's always plenty of time
until it runs out on us
But you can't rush things either
They grow at their own speed
reaching for a point of contact
of their own

I am plagued with impatience
inertia
            the two extremes
the edges of everything
Those two things also
being one

Some people build homes   houses
of themselves   I think of Jung
his circular walls
                        years of
thought enclosing his body
Trapped in his own ideas

Others travel the streets
planting themselves in their
sidewalks
            Their bodies a motion
more like a dance

And some try both worlds
multiple existences
                        are makers of life

Patience is part of it   but more
To have a vision   To make it
real

      Can you see what I'm saying
How time itself is our enemy
our friend   How we trap ourselves
in vision
       But how it also opens
                     out
can lead us forward
How we lose things only to find
them again
         Only to find ourselves
different   at the same place

Listen   this morning the world closes
and opens at my fingertips   The sun
is bright   draws me to it
But I sit in a room cluttered with
memories books old pieces of furniture
old pieces of myself

I am inside
        and outside
of it all
I reach out
with what is behind me
I live my death
       am captured
in my life

LOVE POEM

if I could hold you
if I could wake up in the morning
and see your face
if I could touch you
if I could see you as you go to sleep
if I could feel you close
beside me   if I could reach out to you
touch you   in my need

time drifts endlessly   like water
like this afternoon
the breeze as it drifts
through my window
surrounds me   as thoughts of you
as breath of you
as I see you
as I wait for you
the inevitability of you
as I am surrounded by you
by my love of you
as I waken into life

my words   in silence
my love   in silence
the quiet of the afternoon
the curve of your face
your features   the way
you talk   the way you drift
in my thoughts endlessly
like time

if you were to ask me what defines me
how I place myself in this world
I would say this poem
is the center of it   is the core
that I reach toward the world
as I reach toward you
as one who wants to reach out
endlessly   who wants to open out
endlessly   who wants to feel
endlessly   that question
that is our lives

Cantos for Elegua

CANTOS FOR ELEGUA

I.

Elegua is the guardian of the crossroads
Elegua changes your life   Elegua protects
passageways   what enters and leaves   Elegua
has a knife on his head   It cuts through deception
Scoundrels beware!   Elegua is a trickster
His colors are red and black   The colors of anarchy
revolution

Summon Elegua first with drums and dance and song
It is Elegua who bridges the human and the divine
The Highest   without form or words   speaks through Elegua
Elegua translates many languages   Elegua is a go-between
Elegua is the mouth that devours   his appetite is insatiable
Elegua gives back what he takes   he is generous to a fault

Elegua has the-power-to-make-things-happen
Elegua spins us like a top   Which direction shall we take?
Elegua guides us down paths we would never choose
Elegua teaches us   without him we would be lost
Power lies on the other side of habit   Elegua breaks routine
Elegua kicks you out of bed with one swift kick

Elegua smiles   Elegua has seashells for eyes and mouth
Elegua tucks you in at night   Elegua demands respect
Honor Elegua with caramels and rum
Burn a red candle in his name

II.

Elegua translates words of power   knowing full well
those who carry language bear the brunt
of what they speak   The burden of meaning

is thrust upon them   Should I then refuse words
embrace instead sweet Asphodel like
Williams   or the darker nightmare vision
of a Baudelaire   his flowers of sin

and shame   or should I start with the way
your hand felt   as it carelessly brushed mine
How I wanted to hold it   tight   against me
Nothing is as simple as it seems   The way letters flow

one into the other   their shape   what they signify
A street lamp   thick with soot   Icicles on a branch
heavy with the weight of water frozen to its
spine   All these are words like any other

In the beginning   the word was spoken
into the void   And from that sound came life
Mortals   even gods   can turn their backs on meaning

voice senseless phrases   nonsense syllables
pass them off for speech   but Elegua is not fooled
All ceremonies begin   and end   with him

INCANTATION

Of course   how could it be any different
our first encounter   what goes in the mouth
what comes out   in the way of words
or love   No day is new   we carry years into each dawn
Where is the detail in all this   who bears its name
We are human beings   a people who herd
Burdened with imagination wonder
we keen into the night   The joke's on us
played out by the greatest trickster of them all
An open mouth can never be filled   Emptiness is pure
desire   The language of the gods is food

RETURN

How many years has it been since snow has fallen
as it does tonight   as flakes drift down   now gentle
then brisk   carried by an ever quickening breeze
What is it in us that responds to such a scene
pins the label 'beauty' on this night

Because I cannot speak to you aloud   I conceal
my words in parables poems   in rhythm image metaphor
lines of verse   In a silence built of years and arms

What is it inside me that you touch   What is it
inside me   that responds out of all proportion to
your touch   Beyond desire   the instinct to survive
All that is physical and bound to seasons

Star ships do not fly   They fall up into the cosmos
explode into the universe   Their every instinct to
rebound to earth   as they reluctantly tear free
As gravity holds us all in place   makes every side
right-side-up   as we circle space

There is no detail here   no physical trace
Snow hides everything without discrimination
The magic lies in understanding the secret of return
of falling back   as well as breaking free

OPENING STANZAS

It is harder to write of what
is complete
than what is empty
                We tend
to fill in spaces
avoid confrontation
with meaning
outside ourselves

It is the smell of my room
of what has passed between us
that moves me
Not these words
                or the dozens
I have discarded

How can I say what is contained for me
in the fold of your lip
The way your body leans
                when you dance

What one remembers finally
are the small things
The tangible remains:
a list (unfinished)   a bottle
of perfume   two magazines
a pair of boots
a row of vitamins on the
kitchen shelf

The daisies
I bought you   balanced
lightly   against blue glass

My past rests on the surfaces
of my mind   For me now
the only reality is
our present/presence
together

You fled the seasons
wound up in L.A.
a city I had deserted
years before
        In New York
I welcomed snow as miracle
The way one accustomed to endless day
(where things pass constantly
but never change)
          welcomes
the miracle of night

There are no words adequate for it
For what is between us
They will come later
These are   after all   only
opening stanzas
        welcome as miracle
As I welcome you
pressing against me
draining my emptiness
As together we re-awaken meaning
in small things

                    For you
perhaps   in the seasons
As through you
                    I burst forth
once more
into the sun

TESTAMENT

The age you welcome with
so much grace I wonder at
Granted the wrinkles
deepening on my face
were there at ten
At thirty
        they were fuller
And now   two decades later
show themselves
even in repose
          having begun
to grow   to propagate
themselves
independent of mood

If sometimes now
I settle too quickly
in front of the TV
Pick up a favorite book
instead of grappling
with the day's events
The reason's this:

Years pass
too quickly
I wonder if we ever
really age
       only look
in wonder   from some
unknown space

As around us
the world grows young

FROM NICARAGUA A GIFT

for Margaret Randall

If you were to ask me
to name a color for that land
I would say it was green
But the color you sent was yellow
A plane descending into green
The sun rising golden beyond its wings

Many things are made of gold
A voice sometimes is known as golden
A wedding ring
                Even silence
(when chosen)

But "to be silenced"
That's a different matter
That's to choke on one's own words
erupt in violence
                an act of war

Margaret   today   in your letter
folded in a press release
COVERT ACTIONS AGAINST NICARAGUA
CHALLENGED BY INTERNATIONAL LAW
a small shard of foil falls out
slips to the floor
                I can't make it out
It puzzles me
What is it? What does it say?
A rectangular shape   in the center

a golden face
circled by yellow   edged by red
—a cigar band—
                        a cigar band?
Sol Habana
The Havana Sun

Margaret   in the midst of war
both yours & ours
How my country is trying to silence yours
How the silences here are many
& growing
                & the violence
not limited by nationality borders names

How people are more and more refusing
to be silenced
                    in both our lands
Margaret   in the midst of war
from your letters of anger
                        & triumph
death struggle hope
you have sent me/shared with me
perhaps even as an afterthought
who knows?
                (& I will treasure it always)
a gift of light

ELEGY

for Réne Vallejo Ortiz
1920 - 1969

If I could invoke the dead
I would invoke you
Even the memories of you
I have buried in my heart

You saw in your land
something I could not see
Perhaps because it was so simple
& you were   above all
a simple man

You wrote me: I don't understand
if you feel like it why you don't sit down
and write   You made it sound so easy
& in a way   so true

You told me how healthy you were
How every weekend you rested
How I needed to learn to be like you
& then you died   knowing things are often
not as simple   as they seem

It could almost be a joke
We could laugh at it together
The way we laughed at everything
I told you   It has taken me a long time
to write this poem
& I am beginning to learn

Your death helped me part
of the way   As your life
helped me another   I see each day
how things die   how they leave us empty

I see you as being
even in death   so full of life
& such a simple man

WORDS

              I am trapped
by words
              The ones I speak
The ones I never say

My head stuffed full of dreams
My body of memories
                         I flounder
              between two worlds
The future and the past

I wanted to write a poem
more full of passion   more full
of love
              than any
                       I have ever
              written

How does one measure years
What standard does one use
to weight them
                       I am trapped
              by time
It circles my wrists
                         guides
              my steps

I live in the shadow of my words
They measure the moments
              of my life

What part in all this do you have
What part in all this do I
To understand that question

to hold it
            open
                        to hold it
                                    open
until finding it
we enter
            free

BARCELONA JOURNAL

I.

The hill is on fire. Orange rims it like the sun. It is such a clear
day you can see the city in all directions. Houses poured into
hills, until the hills themselves are really no more than waves
of houses, frozen in cement, tile & brick—the color of muted
earth. Ten miles away the hill is on fire & you can begin, even
here, to smell smoke on the wind. People arrive with binoculars,
telescopes. I have not seen it so clear for days. Buildings curve
round into the sea. A border of dirt and sea. But now all eyes are
directed toward the mountain. The crescent of orange fire barely
visible through the smoke. The sun burns into my back. The other
fire. That Spanish flame.

II.

Alien. There is no other word for it. For the first time, today,
traveling this country road outside Barcelona, I realize I am away,
far away, from home. All cities are in some respects the same.
But here among grass and trees and hills and that strange
mountain range, I feel the difference. Not as being estranged,
divorced from, but as something stronger, something alien.
Something unlike anything I have ever experienced before.

III.

These sudden rains. Not tropical—with lightning, thunder, great
release after hours of tension. But more nonchalant, more
"by-the-by." As if the clouds, rushing to get somewhere else,
were to drop some rain in passing. And so it goes all day.
First dark, then light, then dark, then light. A spotted day. Cool,
but even a slow walk will bring perspiration. It is warm. No,

that's not the word for it. Not cool, not warm. Tepid. The day
is tepid. & slides by.

IV.

PORTRAIT OF BOY, MAN & HORSE

How would they feel
if they knew they formed the subject
of this portrait?
The only color the color
the boy's banging makes
against a large tin plate
What are they selling?
The odd shapes lining three sides
of a wooden crate tell nothing
hold their secret tight as glass
(sea-aged)
           The kind I held yesterday
at the shore
They remind me somehow of the sea
All motion and sound
On the surface thick
                almost monotonous
covering subtler shades
& deeper tones

V.

Time. I think on the way to the park of time. Of how, at the
same instant, I feel both the extension and the lack of it. As if
there were a moment, somewhere, hidden, that if touched would
open the heart of the world to me. And then, turning my head,
I see the hills, so green, so full, they seem without time, without
extension. I see the broken bottle in front of me as part of it.

A piece of mirror: a small black ant. A breeze so gentle it is almost indistinguishable from the movement of children racing by. An edge of clouds. And the sun. The sun! It's very heat forcing me finally to turn away.

VI.

Am I, at last, learning to let things be? To sit and be in this place without fantasy or thought (the wish to be somewhere else, in another place.) I recognize this as something very dear, very precious. When I move, must I lose it? Must even this perception remain in its own place? Can I carry it with me? Can I become it? Oh, if only I could become it. If only I could turn myself into this space.

VII.

JARDINERIA Y CONSTRUCCIONES MITJANS, S.A.

So it says on the side of the giant van
parked by two vehicles, the kind you use to
   flatten roads —
deserted — it being 3 o'clock
   the workmen out to lunch —
2 boys have taken over —
dressed identically in blue-stripped
    shirts —
They tug at levers, shout
   commands neither I nor
    the machine understand —
& in their minds, a road is built,
   a city, an empire,
until their father arrives, short, stout
    & angry

like a brisk north wind,
    & chases them away —

VIII.

It is too hard to explain yourself to other people. Too tiring.
I imagine long speeches. Never delivered. Or if begun, much
less interesting to the person of flesh than to the creatures of my
imagination. I speak of New York, a topic which never much
interested me before, as if the city and I were one. As if by
explaining how I live, where I eat, go to dance, have fun, what
kind of friends I have I explain myself. It is not the city, but me,
I want them to know. But I can never show them how I receive
this world, what kind of person I really am, except, perhaps, by
chance—with a touch, or a poem.

IX.

The real proof of what a person is like is how they act toward
you when you are somehow at their mercy. How parents act with
their children: how lovers act & friends. The measure being what
is at stake. The test of a person—how they use power. How they
abuse or refuse control.

X.

How small everything is. This old villa, only three hundred years
ago, a dwelling place. People lived here, moved around these
rooms from day to day, doing things people did then (and now).
But the wax figures of these people, the old man bent over his
desk, the mother with her candlesticks, the soldier writing orders,
are so small. And their clothing, thick, hand-sewn, is awkward,
graceless. I can't get used to this house, or these people. I try to

place myself back—what it must have been like. But size stops me, not time. This one small woman, no more than shoulder height, clothed in grey and blue, her hand resting gently on a table, looking silently into space.

XI.

The picture of Franco on the coins is gradually being replaced. A main thoroughfare no longer "Generalissimo Franco" (as on all the maps) is now called simply "Diagonal." It is hard for me to imagine what it must have been like here five years ago. Politics seems so far from me in this place. It waits for me at home, in my own language. If you can ever really leave it. The decisions. The implications. But here, now, for me, in the summer air, at least this one afternoon, an interval. A break.

XII.

There are no rules for it. I must learn how to move. I, who having moved too much, have never really learned to leave. A fish moves from tail to fin across great currents guided only by the way the water feels, its weight. But I cannot escape even one moment from myself. I bring all of it with me. Another day. In a different place. I glide by for two months, an instant. I do not even, as others, give the illusion of being here. Where am I then? If not here? Oh, Barcelona, how much you bring me home.

TEN YEARS AFTER

1

How does one find words to speak the things that are too large
for words. How does one fit an idea into a page, a feeling into a
syllable. A room is not a world. A city is not a continent. These
streets do not border the edges of a universe. But the people
who move in them, the people who live in them are a world, a
continent, a universe.

There were things I never learned, even though I began, a little,
to reach out, to believe I could reach out.

Ten years. What does it mean? Ten years. *Elegua.* Guardian of
the Paths, Opener of the Doors. Trickster. The Juggler. The Bal-
ance. The Fool. The way the world goes past our understanding,
resolves itself in our blood. How we play out our days, something
very great, and something very small.

The image of the sea comes too often. The city is another voice.
My own body a boundary harder to resolve. Life is a series
of choices. By which we include or exclude all we ever hoped for
or dreamed of. Love is a series of choices, by which we include
or exclude the world.

2

If I could speak in the images of dream. If I could play the words,
stretch them across a mile of thought. Say it has been so long
since I have allowed myself to feel that now I feel too much.

But the words of a poem are silent, make no sound. Reach across
space hands cannot touch. Part of me has grown old seeing how
people move. At different intervals. At different speeds.

Sometimes, at night, when I am alone, I hear a voice that calls my name. I am haunted by the memory of every person I have ever known, will ever know. I am haunted by the presence of every person I have ever loved, will ever love.

If I could mold myself into a poem, shape myself into a syllable, a group of words. What would it mean?

My memories are ghosts which surround me as I write. My future lies before me like a kind of space. I would ask for a different sense of timing from the world, knowing full well, at that moment, time itself would end and motion cease.

3

What does it mean to lose. To invest in loss. To invest in the possibility of loss.

We move from a sense of need. Both others and our own. But what we move toward is what moves us most.

The wasted days, the wasted hours, the piles of waste that make up much of our lives, that are part of our lives. The time lost. The time spent. The time destroyed.

I want to wake up. Rise up. I want to be awake. To see.

I had almost forgotten what it was like to be next to someone, to be warmed by them. To feel warm. I think of death, more than anything else, as a very cold place. As a place where contact ceases, where a world ends.

I know what it is to lose contact. To see the world grow smaller and smaller. To be unable to reach out. To be unable to speak. I know what death is like, what it means.

As everything begins to fall away.

4

I would like to write a poem that could solve the world,
could solve my place in it. Could make my fantasies into
something real. But I know a poem, words, even these words,
as they come, from my pen, as they sing, as the poem always
sings, as words are used, as motion, as change.

I know a poem can do none of these things.

Cannot stop the minutes, cannot turn even one hour,
cannot bring into being what does not exist.

Because in all these years, with all this strength that has
grown up in me. With all these words that have grown up
in me. I still cannot find speech to say what it is I feel,
when I really care.

5

If a poem were a hand, if it were alive, warm. If it could
reach out. If it could enter places I cannot. If it could do things
that make me afraid.

There is this thing that changes, that allows change to exist.
The poem is part of it, is its voice, this thing that is.

Any struggle is first that deep feeling that grows from
the center of a person, a people. The poem is not separate from
me, from the person I am. It is not the poem, but I, who feels.
It is not the poem, but I, who loves.

To hope, to have hope, to be hopeful, to hope against hope,
to believe in change, to believe in the possibility of change,
to know when to stay. And when to leave.

6

To discover people is to discover a world. To find out what
is important and what is not.

What does it mean to open yourself, to become open, to feel.
What does it mean to open yourself to other people, to allow
them to enter, to allow them to become part of your life.

The mountain stands still; above it fire flames up and does
not tarry. Strange lands and separation are the wanderer's lot.

I am driven by love, *Elegua*. I am driven by love. I cover my
madness, *Elegua*. I cover my pain. Make a place for me in
your house.

Elegua. Elegua. Guardian of the Doors.
Opener of the Paths.

Cover my years. *Elegua.* Cover my years.

Copia divina, en quien veo desvanecido al pincel

The Light that Puts an End to Dreams

A Suite of Poems for
Sor Juana Inés de la Cruz
1651? – 1695

Photographs by Joséphine Sacabo

In the 17ᵗʰ Century a nun defied tradition to become
one of Mexico's greatest scholars and poets.

…my inkwell is the simple pyre
where I set myself aflame.

—*Sor Juana Inés de la Cruz*

I.

Imagine a room   small   squat   windowless
day indistinguishable from night   a single candle burning
a stack of pages   a quill   ink   Imagine a woman
her habit   black   Imagine a woman writing
bent over her desk   her outline barely visible   her face
hidden   Imagine a silence so dense it seems to breathe
Imagine a woman seated inside it   her only illumination
a candle's flame   Imagine the noise of a pen faintly
against parchment   barely penetrating the silence
Imagine everything is still   the arm has stopped
moving   the pen words poems   Imagine a woman
praying   bent over her work   arms outstretched
hands taut with words   Her secret prayer to be relieved
of silence   The answer to her prayer silence
and more silence   Imagine the darkness growing
until the figure of the woman disappears
the words   the candle's flame   Imagine a silence
without color   without interruption   respite
an infinite silence   Imagine the loneliness of such a
silence   The infinite loneliness of such a silence

Los Volcanes

II.

Pyramids   cylinders   the abstract body of the mind
colliding into forms   haunting your dreams   stripping
your bones of desire   your waking body shrouded forever
Narcissus caught in the first reflection   consumed by
love   It is not his face that betrays him   sparks
his lust   that beautiful boy   but the way his hand floats
gently   across the skin of the water   fingers tangled soft
within its touch   Even so God   His breath stirring
the depths   seduced by the waters   needing someone
tangible to love Him   a reflection   He could see Himself
mirrored in   could make Him real   It was the motion
of the waters that drew him (that drew Him)
that compelled him (Him) to plunge into its depths
to sink into the outstretched arms   the hands
that touched his own shining from the darkness
Those arms   those soft cylinders of dream   their cold hard
edges softened by the motion of water slowly
enveloping him   Circles drifting together until everything
became thick to his touch   until finally aware finally
trying to pull away finally struggling to grasp for breath
for breath to breathe he (He) sank

Is this what you saw   Is this what haunted you
This vision of a world that glues us to it   mirror upon
mirror   reflection upon reflection   Plato's world
The world of Maya   illusion   You who had no waking
mirror   but your own mind   to tell you who you were

III.

Because the mind cannot encompass the realm
you sought   Because the body is weak
Because you knew it would never be more than a phantom
a nightmare   irresistible   but terrifying   Because you
longed for it   Because you could never trust you had seen
anything   although you knew with certainty you had
Because your vision came without advice   instruction
Because it was not beautiful   not sensual   fit nothing
you had ever heard or known   brought with it no ecstasy
no revelation   Because you did not know if it would
come again   you constructed a mansion to put it in
a dream palace in verse   Hoping somehow by arranging
stanzas like building blocks like towers like battlements
it would appear to you   you could scale it   the daydreams
of mystics philosophers poets   You discovered your own
frailty   the shortcomings of the human body   mind
The face of God does kill and wound   and maim

Derrumbo

IV.

You looked to God for love   looked to love for God
Denied words you measured objects in your mind
saw the mystical implications behind each syllable
The language of the physical world

It was women you turned to for passion   women
you lay with at night in your poems   hidden behind
stanzas metaphors   phonetic conventions   But it was men
who constructed the ethereal edifices

you longed to inhabit   Pico   Ficino   Bruno
Albertus Magnus   Athanasius Kircher   the Egyptians
Gnostics   It was men you expected to lead you away
from Man

Did you ever touch yourself   *Sor Juana*   wishing it one
of your countesses or queens   Did you ever imagine them
kissing you   lifting those skirts you wore even to bathe
kissing your lips   your breasts   the tender openings

between your legs   Did you ever imagine holding them
knowing through their bodies what was forbidden you
to see in yours   Is there any way you could have imagined
such things   knowing only the crudities of love

the babies that followed after   Was it your passion
that finally betrayed you   *Sor Juana*   Was that
the Truth that sent you into silence   Fearing more than
the strictures of the church   the loss of your own soul

V.

Darkness rises   still unable to penetrate the layer
beneath the sun   has no need   night already reaching
down   earth inevitably turning toward it   Is it really

that layer of night you fear   its dark shroud
growing from earth   slowly spreading   shadows
lengthening until they meet and merge   sending all

creatures but your vigilant eagle to sleep   Darkness
births us   is the source of creativity   art religion
science   Is it possible day is the real adversary

The light that puts an end to dreams

En perseguirme mundo, que interesas?

VI.

Do you still draw the outline of her form   as you lie
pressed against your pillow   as you sit   elegant
even in nuns' robes   surrounded by thousands
of volumes   musical instruments   gifts from
wealthy patrons   Is it her features that haunt you
not your devoted Countess   she whose portrait
graces your ring   your sonnets safe under
her name   The early days at Court

the façade of graceful courtiers   how you excel
youth part of your charm   But you grow older
your body matures   She catches your attention
You speak to her alone without artifice   She replies
It begins   Her speech more beautiful than any
of the mannered words you hear at court
Or is it the way her hands move against the light
You touch   Your hands arms thighs meet

Your mouth finds other uses   You cover yourself
with words   charming those around you   You think
of her   always of her   You are eighteen   old
for marriage   expected roles   There are questions
You choose the Convent   move your court   your books
your circle of friends   your taste for finer things
You move everything you love   but not her not her
but not her

VII.

There are places better left open   unattended
even you must have known that in your heart
your mind busy with answers   and poems

You closed the doors of the world behind you
created your own world out of your
imagination   You say you lived in religion

without religion   yet you searched the soul's path
filled your work with figures of myth and ancient lore
Is it possible the Inquisitors were right   It was all an act

Showing off your learning   A seasoned performer
posturing before her mirror   delighting in the way
her body moves and curls under her manipulation

each step pre-planned   Nothing left to chance
Did you actually believe Bruno's exhortations
Love a snare only in actualization   Never be the lover

The loved one holds the power   Love without
object   knowing only the passion of intellect
The way a Yogi brings himself to climax

then refuses to let go   drawing his energy back
into himself   letting nothing escape
Was that the secret   your poems conceal

not love   but power   Was that the lie
that killed you as you   like Daedalus' son
learned the truth of heat   and flame

VIII.

When galaxies collide stars are formed in sheets of fire
blood red to the eye   a bubble expanding until it bursts
deflates   imploding back into itself   transformed like
sacramental wine   the Eucharist   the blood of Christ
sacrifice of the King   Christian   Aztec   married in
blood   Hearts pierced   torn

like yours   like you   born in blood   bearing blood
monthly reminder of what it means to be
a woman   The mystery of mass   your own
flesh   One ritual sacred   the other   profane

Observe it   your Triumph   borne from your pen
serpent jaguar lizard   flower   bearers of good tidings
and bad   winding in endless procession   crying out for
recognition   faith   the difference between
God   and knowledge

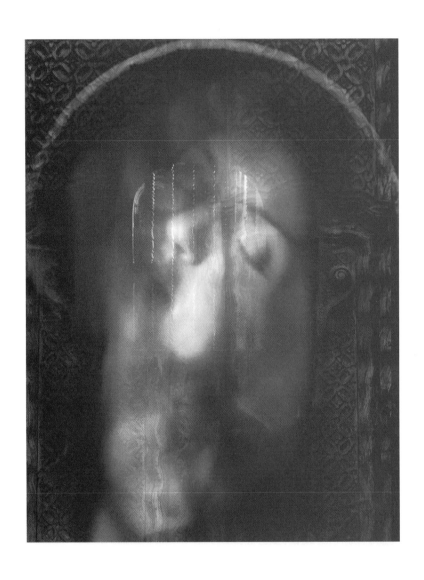

Si te labra prisión mi fantasía

La Pasion

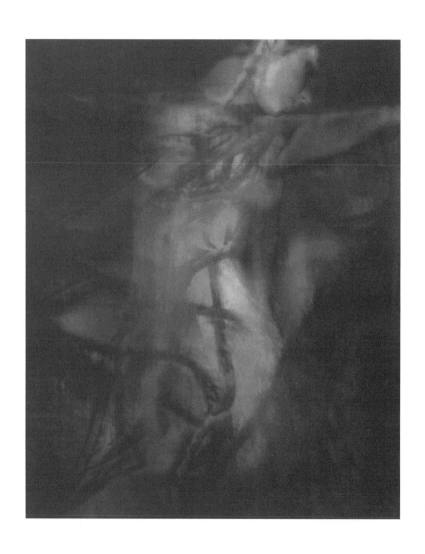

IX.

The graceful portico of your convent   detailed panels
delicately interlocking arcs   spirals   The Order
of St. Jerome   a city unto itself   rows of rectangles
tiers of cells   straight lines   ninety-degree angles

Precise geometry broken only by a scattering
of trees   You maintained your elegance   your servant
Juana de San José   a present from your mother
This was New Spain   not paradise   An immense

country   mimicking the old   north to Florida Texas
San Francisco   south to the sea   you at the center
How many years did it take you to realize where
you were   who you had become   Not square

within square   symbol of the immutable   the wisdom
of intellect   Motion defines us   is what we know
as life   even as our body separates us from air   the food we
breathe   From other creatures   A complex of circles ovals

openings   what gives birth   Your world was women
your days filled by them   until at night   alone   you shut
them out   Did death shatter your last defense   In face of
others' suffering was it human touch you craved

in those last months   Tending your sisters in their illness
as you held them   as you let them hold you   knowing
such love   knowing full well the cost of such love

X.

The plague came   The air she breathed betrayed her
The church which once cajoled now threatened her
Her protectors returned to Spain   The abyss opened
at her feet   Form shattered into chaos   Number had
no meaning   The gods goddesses animals birds the heroes
heroines that colored her poems fell into disarray   Words
crusted her lips   The air reeked of death   Nothing
made sense   She remembered her childhood   She recognized
her longing   She discarded the eloquence of her poems her
essays her plays   She rent her gown   shaved her head
She yearned for order   She signed her confession
with her own blood   She gave up her music her books
She relinquished pride in her accomplishments
She sought in darkness what she had once sought in
light   She prayed for forgiveness   She prayed for mercy
She reached into the abyss   She tended her sisters' needs
She begged her God not to abandon her   She clung to
life   Her consciousness failed   She no longer dreamed

La Muerte

XI.

There is no way to imagine her final hours   what she saw
when she finally descended into that darkness she loved
so well   Desire   once a pawn of intellect   became real
loss made it real   As once she had drawn her own
blood   marveled at its consistency   her confession
flowing onto parchment   The unanswerable
exploding her soul   questions

impossible to grasp   the truth of limitation   the outline
of our bodies as we confront ourselves   *Sor Juana*
What was it like to believe in word as symbol music magic
hieroglyph   Plato and Christ bound together
ungraceful lovers   What is more ephemeral than
words   the pretense of numbers

Sor Juana   Did you try one last time to make
that leap of faith   to purify yourself   to make of
yourself the gold without blemish   reaching for the divine
inside yourself   only to discover once again you were
only human   or did you ultimately succeed
forsaking your last breath   as you finally let go

EPILOGUE

Dream now forever in darkness Sor Juana
The fiction you lived   All we know of you
Your words   centuries old   What others wrote
of you   The madness of your times
                                   and ours

NOTES

INTRODUCTION

"I like the word 'origins'…" originally appeared in *We stand Our Ground: Three Women, Their Vision, Their Poems,* by Kimiko Hahn, Gale Jackson, Susan Sherman, with artwork by Josely Carvalho (IKON, 1988, pp. 9-29). Reprinted in *Art on the Line: Essays by Artists about the Point where Their Art & Activism Intersect,* ed. Jack Hirschman (Curbstone Press, 2002, pp. 319-343).

America's Child: A Woman's Journey through the Radical Sixties, Susan Sherman (Curbstone Press/Northwestern University, 2007).

"The Tyranny of Form," "The ABC of Madness—The Legacy of Derrida," "The Obscure Subject of Desire: The Despair of Jacque Lacan," appeared in *The Color of the Heart: Writing from Struggle & Change 1959-1990* (Curbstone Press, 1990).

The seven issues of *IKON,* Series One, were published from February 1967 to February 1969. *IKON,* Series Two, was published from 1982 to 1994.

"In a poem, words…" originally appeared in *With Anger/With Love: Selections Poems & Prose (1963-1972).* Susan Sherman (Mulch Press, 1974, p. vii).

"My hands were perspiring…" *America's Child,* pp. 90-93.

GENESIS

"The Real Questions" was inspired by a Buddhist parable about a man who falls off a cliff and is saved (temporarily at least) by clinging to a branch that juts out from its side. Above him is a lion, below the abyss. But when he sees to one side of him a bunch of bright red strawberries, they appear so beautiful to him he reaches to touch them even though it means he might fall to his death.

"Genesis" was my first prose poem, written around 1962 on the advice of Theodore Enslin who said I should try to write a poem with a longer line to break myself of writing poems that were too condensed.

AREAS OF SILENCE

"First and Last Poems." Violeta Parra was a folklorist, singer/ composer, political progressive, artist. Her music was influential in the "New Song" movement, La Nueva Canción, and her La Peña de Los Parra brought back the tradition of a place for the arts and political action. She committed suicide in 1967, suppos-edly over a broken romance, but she had been under continual pressure and sometimes ridicule as a political activist artist.

This poem was written after a trip to Chile in the early 1970s when Allende was in power. The scenery reminded me of my childhood home in California. Some of the references are to im-ages from the books of Carlos Castañeda.

"The Meeting." My first love poem to a woman. I read it for years without saying that it was written to a woman. It was the poem that led Allen Ginsburg to "out" me.

"Love Poem/ for a Capricorn." I am a Cancer, water. Capricorn, of course, is earth.

"Areas of Silence." My second prose poem written in Manhattan around 1963.

"Reminiscences." Written when I came back from my first Cuba trip in 1968-1969. I found it hard to talk or write about the trip because it affected me so deeply, and then one night Margaret Randall called me from Mexico City. After I spoke to her the poem began to take shape. The pain I mention turned out to be a duodenal ulcer because of which I returned to Cuba the following year for medical attention since I didn't have health insurance and even at that early date couldn't get the medical attention I needed in New York. The East River refers to the river that flows east of Manhattan.

"Lilith of the Wildwood, of the Fair Places." First published in *Liberation Newspaper (The Rat)* in 1970 when it was taken over by the women for a special issue. The Lilith tale was told to me originally by Allen Katzman as an old Jewish Polish fable about how mothers wrote blessings on the walls when they gave birth to keep Lilith from stealing their newborn babies. This was written before Lilith became a fixture in the women's movement. The "outlaws" were also a reference to political women who were living underground at the time.

"A Word to the Wise." Krishnamurti (1895-1986) was a prodigy of Annie Besant, the head of the Theosophical Society. At the age of 32 he renounced ties to any religious organization. He spent the rest of his life teaching that "Truth is a Pathless Land."

"It Was Easier Then." Ho Chi Minh was the president of North Vietnam from 1954-1969, the year of his death. He was called by some "the father of his country."

Haydée Santamaria was one of the women who participated in the attack on the Moncado Barracks on July 26, 1953. She was the head of Casa de las Américas, an important Cuban cultural institution.

George Jackson, the author of *Soledad Brother*, a book of his prison letters from 1964 to 1970, was killed in what the authorities claimed was a prison break in 1971.

Fred Hampton, deputy chairman of the Illinois chapter of the Black Panther Party, was shot to death in his bed by the Chicago police on December 4, 1969.

Rosa Parks in 1955 refused to surrender her seat in the bus to a white passenger which led to the Montgomery Bus Boycott.

Lolita Labrón, an activist in the struggle for Puerto Rican independence, was imprisoned for twenty-five years for her involvement in an attack on the House of Representatives. She was pardoned by Jimmy Carter in 1981 after which she remained active in the fight for independence.

Assata Shakur, one of the targets of the FBI's cointelpro program against the Black Panther Party, escaped from jail in 1979 where she was falsely imprisoned for the "murder" of a police officer after being pulled over by the New Jersey State Police and shot two times.

Martin Luther King and Malcolm X need no footnotes.

"Facts" was written in 1984 while working with the organization Art Against Apartheid with whom *IKON* co-sponsored an anti-apartheid reading and then collaborated on an a special double issue #5/6 of the magazine.

"Letter from Havana." René Vallejo Ortiz was my doctor. I met him at a reception during the Cultural Congress of Havana in January, 1968. When he heard upon my return to New York that I was sick and in need of medical care, he invited me to return to Havana for medical attention. Vallejo, who died on August 13, 1969, spent his life in service to others. In 1945, he organized a hospital in Germany, with the help of the Red Cross, and under the auspices of the UN worked to rehabilitate the victims of World War II. In Cuba, during the revolutionary war, he was arrested by the Batista dictatorship and on his release he joined the rebel army, where he treated wounded rebels and farmers and later saw to the construction of schools and health conferences. He stayed by Fidel's side as his doctor until his death in 1969. This prose poem was written while I was convalescing in Havana.

"We must always remember the complexity of the simple" is a quote from St. Thomas Aquinas.

LONG DIVISION

"Sixth Street Rhapsody" refers to Sixth Street in Manhattan between First and Second Avenues.

"Holding Together" refers to Ave. A in Manhattan, just at the beginning of gentrification. I had an apartment on 9th Street between Aves B & C in the middle 60s.

CANTOS FOR ELEGUA

"Cantos for Elegua." Elegua is the Yoruba Orisha of the Cross-roads. He is the opener of the doors, the messenger of the gods who translates the sacred languages. He is the trickster. In Cuba, he is placed by the side of doorways to protect the home. All ceremonies begin and end with a tribute to him.

"Barcelona Journal." These poems were written in 1977 during a month I spent in Barcelona. I stayed in an apartment on a hill about twenty minutes by bus from downtown, and every day I would go to the park and write.

"Ten Years After." The title of the poem refers to ten years after I left California to live in New York. It was written when I returned from Cuba where I brought home two small images of the orisha Elegua—one of which I gave to a friend in the Yoruba religion who had requested it and the other which, through a series of strange circumstances, wound up with me. Elegua came to represent for me the change in the path my life had taken after I returned from Cuba.

THE LIGHT THAT PUTS AN END TO DREAMS

Photographs By Josephine Sacabo:

Copia divina, en quien veo desvanecido al pincel (Divine image, where I see the spent brush)
Los Volcanes (The Volcanos)
Derrumbo (Ruins)
En persequirme mundo, que interesas? (In persecuting me, world, what interests you?)
La Pasion (Passion)
Si te labra prisión mi fantasía (Your prison in my fantasy)
Lazos (Bindings)
La Muerte (Death)

Sor Juana Inés de la Cruz (1651?-1695): Sor Juana has been proclaimed by many the "first feminist of the Americas." In her famous response "La Respuesta," she defends women's right to study, to write, to teach. Her poem "First Dream" is a compendium of Renaissance philosophy and Hermetic lore. Her love poems to her patronesses continue to be a source of inspiration and controversy. When her patrons, the Viceroy of New Spain and his wife, her beloved María Luisa, returned to Spain, she lost her protection from her enemies in the church. In 1694, under duress, she renewed her vows and entered a period of penance and silence. In 1695, amidst widespread rioting and epidemics, she fell ill while nursing her sisters, and died.

I.

This poem refers to the two years of silence when she was not allowed to teach or study.

II.

 This poem references her poem "First Dream." The world of Maya is the world of illusion.

IV.

 Pico della Mirandola (1463-1494) was a Renaissance philosopher famous for his "Oration on the Dignity of Man," a humanist text that emphasized the importance of the quest for knowledge.

 Marsilio Ficino, a Renaissance humanist philosopher (1493-1499), was Pico's teacher. He translated Plato's works into Latin and was a great supporter of revival of the Liberal Arts.

 Giordano Bruno (1548-1600) was burned at the stake for heresy and refusing to totally recant his liberal ideas about the universe and religion, embracing the ideas of Copernicus. He is also noted for his work with memory.

 Albertus Magnus (1193-1280) was a German philosopher and theologian. He was also rumored to be a magician and alchemist. He believed that there was no dichotomy between science and religion. A Dominican, he was Thomas Aquinas' teacher. He was made a Saint in 1931.

 Athanasius Kircher (1602-1680), a German Jesuit scholar, was a true Renaissance man studying such diverse topics and Egyptian hieroglyphs, writing an encyclopedia of China, working with microorganisms and magnets. His work is illustrated by elaborately detailed drawings.

V.

 This poem also references "First Dream" and ideas inspired by Pablo Neruda's poem "I Ask for Silence" from *Extravagaria*, translated by Alastair Reid.

VI.

 This is an "Imaginary" poem.

VII:

In the myth Daedalus builds wings made of feathers and wax and warns his son Icarus not to fly too high because the heat of the sun could melt the wax. Icarus doesn't obey his father, flies too high, his wings melt and he falls to his death.

VIII.

"Triumph" is a play on the word meaning victory as well as its Renaissance meaning of a medieval procession.

IX.

The Viceroyalty of New Spain lasted from approximately 1535 to 1821. A viceroy who lived in Mexico City governed the territory, which included (among other regions) Mexico, the Southwestern United States, California, Central America, Florida and the Caribbean.

XI.

"Gold without blemish" refers to the gold produced by the alchemical process. Alchemy is the subject of many of the texts read by Sor Juana including those of Athanasius Kircher.

ACKNOWLEDGMENTS

Quote at front of book: Paul Virilio interviewed by Louise K. Wilson in *Electronic Culture* (Timothy Druckery, ed., Aperture Foundation, 1996, p. 328).

"…my inkwell is the simple pyre/ where I set myself aflame" is a translation of a fragment of a poem by Sor Juana by Electra Arenal and Amanda Powell from Sor Juana Ines de la Cruz, *The Answer/LaRespuesta* (The Feminist Press at the City University of New York, 1994, p. 177).

Some of the work contained in the present volume has appeared in previous books by Susan Sherman, including: *America's Child: A Woman's Journey through the Radical Sixties; We stand Our Ground: Three Women, Their Vision, Their Poems; With Anger/With Love: Selections Poems & Prose (1963-1972), Women Poems Love Poems; The Color of the Heart: Writing from Struggle and Change 1959 - 1990; With Anger/With Love; Shango de Ima.*

Some poems have appeared in the following magazines and anthologies: *13th Moon; Affilia; A Gathering of the Tribes; An Ear to the Ground; Amazon Poetry; American Poetry Review; Art Against Apartheid: Works for Freedom; Bridges; Changer L'Amérique:Anthologie de la Poésie Protestataire des USA (1980-1995); Conditions; Downtown Poets; El Corno Emplumado; Heresies; IKON; Learning Our Way; Lesbian Culture: An Anthology; LibeRATion Newspaper; Local Knowledge; Long Shot; Malpaís Review; Mulch; Poetry Like Bread; Sinister Wisdom; The Arc of Love: An Anthology of Lesbian Love Poems; The Café Review; The Nation; Women Brave in the Face of Danger*

MARGARET RANDALL is a feminist poet, writer, photographer and social activist. Born in New York City in 1936, she has lived for extended periods in Albuquerque, New York, Seville, Mexico City, Havana, and Managua. Shorter stays in Peru and North Vietnam were also formative. In the turbulent 1960s, she co-founded and co-edited *El Corno Emplumado / The Plumed Horn*, a bilingual literary journal which for eight years published some of the most dynamic and meaningful writing of the era. In 2004 she was the first recipient of PEN New Mexico's Dorothy Doyle Lifetime Achievement Award for Writing and Human Rights Activism. In 2009 two of her photographs were accepted into the Capitol Arts Foundation permanent collection of work by New Mexican artists on display at the New Mexico State capitol. Among Randall's more than 100 published books, some of the most recent are *Stones Witness* (The University of Arizona Press); *To Change The World: My Years In Cuba* (Rutgers University Press); *Their Backs To The Sea* and *Our Town* and *As If the Empty Chair / Como si la silla vacía* (Wings Press); *First Laugh* (University of Nebraska Press); *Something's Wrong with the Cornfields* (Skylight Press); and *Ruins* (University of New Mexico Press).

For more information, go to: www.margaretrandall.org

JOSÉPHINE SACABO lives and works mostly in New Orleans, where she has been strongly influenced by the unique ambience of the city. She is a native of Laredo, Texas, and was educated at Bard College, New York. Previous to coming to New Orleans, she lived and worked extensively in France and England. Her earlier work was in the photo-journalistic tradition, influenced by Robert Frank, Josef Koudelka, and Henri Cartier-Bresson. She now works in a very subjective, introspective style. She uses poetry as the genesis of her work and lists poets as her most important influences, among them Rilke, Baudelaire, Pedro Salinas, and Vincente Huidobro. Besides being extensively shown in the United States, her work has been shown in galleries around the world including London, Paris, Guatemala, Brussels, Madrid, Mexico. Her work appears in many books, including a reissue of the classic Mexican novel by Juan Rulfo, *Pedro Páramo* (University Of Texas and the Wittliff Collection of Southwestern and Mexican Art, 2002), which contains 50 of her photographs. Her work appears in the permanent collection of numerous museums, including: Houston Museum of Fine Arts; New Orleans Museum of Art; Wittliff Collection of Southwestern and Mexican Art, San Marcos, Texas; Metropolitan Museum of Art; Museum of Modern Art and the Whitney Museum of American Art.

For more information, go to: www.josephinesacabo.com

SUSAN SHERMAN: Poet, playwright, essayist, editor and co-founder of IKON magazine, she has had twelve plays produced off-off-Broadway, has published four collections of poetry and an adaptation of a Cuban play by Pepe Carril, *Shango de Ima* (Doubleday, 1971) which won 11 AUDELCO awards for a 1996 revival produced by the Nuyorican Poets Café. Noted Historian Blanche Wiesen Cook calls her book of collected essays and poems, *The Color of the Heart: Writing from Struggle & Change, 1959-1990* (Curbstone), "...a powerful and sensitive picture of our history no informed reader should be without." Her latest book *America's Child: A Woman's Journey through the Radical Sixties* (Curbstone, November 2007) has garnered critical acclaim from the *New York Times Book Review, Booklist, Publishers Weekly* and *Lambda Book Review* and numerous authors, including Grace Paley, Claribel Alegria and Chuck Wachtel.

Her awards include a 1997 fellowship from the New York Foundation for the Arts for Creative Nonfiction Literature, a 1990 NYFA fellowship for Poetry, a Puffin Foundation Grant

(1992), a Creative Artist's Public Service (CAPS) poetry grant (1966) and editors' awards from the Coordinating Council of Literary Magazines (CCLM) and the New York State Council on the Arts (NYSCA).

Originally from California, she moved to New York in 1961 where she became artistically and politically active. In the 1960s she was poetry editor and a theater critic for *The Village Voice* and ran the open readings along with Allen Katzman and Carol Berge at the Metro Café. She traveled to Cuba in 1968 to attend the Cultural Congress of Havana and returned there for an extended stay a year later. She taught at the Free University of New York and the Alternate U., co-founded and edited *IKON* magazine and opened IKON bookstore which served as a cultural and movement center.

In 1970 she was involved in the Fifth Street Women's Building squatter's action, after which she became active in the feminist movement and the gay liberation movement. In 1971 she traveled to Chile while Allende was still in power. In 1975 she taught at the feminist institute Sagaris and in 1984 attended a conference on Central America in Nicaragua and revived *IKON* as a feminist magazine. After almost twenty years, she returned to Cuba in the 1990s as part of a feminist trip organized by Margaret Randell.

Among other periodicals and anthologies, her work has been published in *Changer L'Amérique: Anthologie de la Poésie Protestataire des USA (1980-1995)*, *The Arc of Love*, *An Ear to the Ground*, *Poetry (Chicago)*, *The American Poetry Review*, *The Nation*, *Conditions*, *A Gathering of the Tribes*, *El Corno Emplumado*, and *Heresies*.

She is currently working on *Nirvana on Ninth Street*—her first book of fiction—and *The Counterfeit Revolution: The Future by Design*. She teaches part-time at Parsons The New School of Design.

For more information, go to: www.susansherman.com.

Colophon

This first edition of *The Light that Puts an End to Dreams,* by Susan Sherman, has been printed on 70 pound coated paper at Edwards Brothers Printing, Ann Arbor, Michigan. Book and section titles have been set in Aquiline Two type, the text in Adobe Caslon type. All Wings Press books are designed and produced by Bryce Milligan, publisher and editor.

On-line catalogue and ordering:
www.wingspress.com

Wings Press titles are distributed
to the trade by the
Independent Publishers Group
www.ipgbook.com
and in Europe by
www.gazellebookservices.co.uk

Also available as an ebook.